sors and students. My doctoral advisor and I vividly recalled the above editorial transgressions many decades later. My former supervisor did not report taking any specific action in response, other than to stress to us with the example that such actions were wrong. Perhaps in the context, an earlier time and different place, he had no real choices. In my case, also many decades ago, I did not confront the editor, although in retrospect I think I should have. However, I never again submitted papers to that editor. I told my students that I thought the editor's decision was wrong, but sometimes editors, like anyone else, are not always perfect in their exercise of authority. I assured the students whose work was rejected in that unprofessional manner that I would work with them to see their work incorporated into later products that would be submitted elsewhere for review.

Imagine that one of your advisees is a teaching assistant or instructor and suspects that a student has incorporated someone else's text in a term paper without proper credit. Most universities have prescribed procedures for addressing a suspected breach of academic integrity. Checking the regulations together and referring the case to the appropriate body is easy. The part not usually explained in any instructors' handbook is how the graduate teaching assistant should handle continuing interactions with the suspected cheater. Will the graduate assistant later need extra encouragement to teach or assist in another course? What should advisors do if, in retaliation, the suspected violator posts untrue negative personal or professional comments on a social media or professorial rating website, while the student-instructor remains bound by strict rules of confidentiality? There may be further disciplinary options, but it is very difficult to expunge data, accurate or false, from the World Wide Web or anonymous course evaluations. Systems vary widely, and there is no best answer. But nobody on campus is likely closer to the graduate student than the advisor, and the central duty of guiding a dissertation must be expanded to providing moral support and helping engage the available institutional supports (e.g., student services, academic integrity, legal aid, or Internet security).

I had several meetings with a prospective doctoral student about possible thesis topics and the need to become more competitive for fellowships. One of my first questions was whether her master's thesis from another university contained publishable material. She had been assigned part of a series of projects with her advisor, to which she added new insights; the thesis content could not be said to be uniquely the intellectual property of one or the other. If a thesis is submitted and accepted, the student is at least part owner of the contents—or the advisor should be granted another degree. But she mentioned that the advisor, with whom she maintained a cordial personal relationship, had published a paper incorporating parts of the thesis without crediting her as a coauthor. I expressed a strong opinion that this was wrong. Many universities have a stated policy that a student is normally the primary author of work emanating from the dissertation and the advisor is an appropriate coauthor. Together we discussed how to communicate this to her past advisor without risking their relationship, and how to generate a publication benefit for the prospective student. We located the paper online, and indeed this applicant was not even acknowledged. We discussed what other results might be worthy of publication and identified one. I suggested that she e-mail the past advisor, mention that she had read the paper drawn from the thesis, and suggest an additional paper of which she would be the first joint author, prepare the first draft, incorporate his comments, and make the formal submission. The advisor responded quickly and agreed.

This was a lesson in gentle persuasion for the student; it affirmed her rightful authorship and enabled her to put a relationship that she valued back on the rails. The student and advisor had been on good terms, but the student felt cheated. I suspect that her normally thoughtful advisor, who had overstepped an academic integrity boundary, understood the message. The outcome in such attempts is not always positive, however. Another student I know had collected master's thesis data, and the advisor published an abstract based on some of those data. The program director said not to rock the boat—not appropriate advice—so the student changed thesis topics.

Advisors must not present students' ideas as their own. They sometimes do so unintentionally as the outcome of a close and sharing relationship; my wife has at times reminded me that it was she, not I, who made some clever suggestion! But it is not always benign. Advisors expect acknowledgment of sources by students and must reciprocate. The best prevention is frank communication and notes, if not formal minutes, of meetings. With my permission, one of my students voice-recorded every meeting to facilitate her review; if questions arose later, this would provide powerful evidence of who suggested what. During one-on-one meetings I have many times said to other students, "Why aren't you taking notes?" My intent was to make sure good ideas were not forgotten. In retrospect, such notes can also protect students' intellectual property.

If a student suspects that an advisor has stolen his or her ideas, then there are formal procedures to follow, but fear of retribution, financial dependence, and need for reference letters will impel most students to take no formal action, and perhaps not even to complain to their friends. Given the imbalance in power, advisors must be proactive and transparent in honoring students' intellectual property, even when it is shared.

Other academic situations we might face together include a student's incompletely crediting reference material (the first time this happens, especially in a draft, advisors should treat it as a learning moment) or exceeding the boundaries in data collection. For example, one of my doctoral students had ethics approval to voice-record a group of children and their teacher working together, but another teacher sat in one day and was also recorded. The graduate student did not know what to do. My advice was to get after-the-fact consent and report the incident to the ethics board; had an ethics amendment not been approved, we would have edited out the additional person.

Unethical behavior extends beyond the usual categories addressed in academic behavior codes. Key examples include respecting confidences shared by students, never gossiping about students or colleagues, being honest, and handling grant and university money with special care. A reputation for integrity can be earned in a career and lost in a tweet.

Time Counts

Advisors are usually generous in sharing their expertise. However, accessibility, availability, responsiveness, and realistically assessing the time needed to do research or complete other obligations remain high on student priority lists of compliments and complaints. Dealing well with time conveys respect. The impact of contacting a student who has not been in touch for several weeks is frequently heard in testimonials to advisors who receive awards for their work with students. For decades I have exchanged a signed contract with every advisee, containing mutual commitments including some related to time (see appendix 2).

Yet anecdotes abound about graduate students who cannot get comments on drafts, proposal-defense dates, recommendation letters, or replies to e-mails. I recall more than one supervisor with a reputation for taking months to read draft texts. Yes, advisors can be very busy, some students are too dependent, and some students make poor progress and then expect quick feedback to a large chunk of long-overdue material, such as a full dissertation draft. Allocating fault, however, does not resolve the problem. Needlessly making students cool their heels is either mean-spirited or inconsiderate. It does not teach any useful lessons. It is a form of punishment, and punishment is most effective at causing avoidance. Supervisors need to break the pattern.

ACCESSIBILITY

Accessibility is about being reasonably easily and conveniently contactable for short questions, signatures, and setting appointments. A colleague's student was sending e-mails, then texting minutes later wondering why the advisor had not yet replied. The good news was that the advisor was accessible and was perceived by her student as such. The bad news was that they lacked reasonable mutual expectations about the time frame for a reply or criteria to distinguish an important message from an urgent one. Relationships can benefit from occasional renegotiation. All students, especially those who elect the famous-researcher or pedigree advising model, need to anticipate that their advisors might travel frequently or reside elsewhere as visiting scholars. Advisors should keep students informed about when they will be away and how they can be contacted. If there will be interruptions in accessibility and constraints on time, it is our obligation to ensure that someone else on campus is available to intervene—for example, a committee member or coadvisor. A very clear understanding is needed between the substituting advisor and the original advisor—depending on when actual work on the thesis begins—that the work initiated with one or the other is to be continued, encouraged, and guided. I know a case in which the student started serious thesis work with a replacement advisor, and then the returning original advisor rejected all the work done with the sabbatical replacement and forced the student to begin again. At the same time, absence from campus is less of a handicap than it was in the past, given the availability of Skype, virtual meeting, and editing tools on many sorts of devices.

AVAILABILITY

I find it useful to distinguish between being accessible or contactable and being available. It is possible to be accessible and respond rapidly to e-mails, for example, but to have great difficulty finding a time to meet with a student. Availability is about being around for formally scheduled and the occasional informal or casual conversation, but also about establishing clear expectations with every student about how often and how long to meet, and adjusting that frequency and interval to shifting student needs. Availability can be in person or virtual; even a required signature can be easily scanned or faxed. As dean of students and in my occasional ensuing role as acting ombudsperson for students, I met graduate students from many disciplines who had not interacted with their advisors for months. Some had tried; others were too timid to try. Unless the student is unresponsive, more than a couple of months without at least some form of extended discourse from an advisor appears delinquent.

During a sabbatic year at a British institute, I discovered that, at the time, graduate students in that institution were allotted a fixed ration of advising hours. Once these were used up, the student was on his or her own. Whether hours are formally fixed by institutional design or decided by the professor's whim, students should be informed about what and how much assistance to seek from their primary advisor, and about any limits to those interactions. The advising quota was unusual, but it reminded advisors that they were obligated to make those hours available to their students and that students should make the most of them. The underlying idea is sound: students and advisors must together make efficient use of advisory time; students must be told it is their responsibility to book the time, and advisors must make the time available.

Students are likely to complain to fellow students about low availability before telling their advisors. Related issues are being on time for meetings and not missing meetings—in the age of mobile devices with alarm functions, text messages, social networks, and e-mail, no student or advisor should ever be stood up.

RESPONSIVENESS

Timely feedback—under two weeks for major sections of text, a week in the normal course of events, and two days if possible—is respectful, builds trust, and enables students to remember what they are getting the feedback about. It is fair to tell students that they should discuss with you the points at which they will submit substantial items for your feedback and to set a hoped-for response time, then to put the item in our agenda. If the student's submission deadline is missed, the advisor may have other commitments that take priority in the new time frame, and it is appropriate to indicate such delays. However, long gaps waste students' valuable time because they must wait before proceeding. Intentional long gaps are punitive. It is fair, however, to negotiate a longer delay if students can make parallel progress on other responsibilities. It is also fair, when a student has missed several deadlines when time had been set aside to provide feedback, to impose a delay of weeks or even a few months in order to address other commitments—renewing a research grant, for example, on which many students depend for their livelihood.

Of equal consequence, students need explicit feedback about what is good in their work and what can be better, as well as what changes are desirable and which are essential. It is not helpful or fair merely to place a check-mark on some pages. It is worse to strike out chunks of text or to fill the margins with question marks. Every response to each student submission is part of constructive mentoring toward real colleagueship. Advising is a special kind of inquiry-driven learning in which one of the explicit goals is that advisors' roles can be taken up by students when they graduate, and part of the progression toward this outcome is that we gradually come to learn from them. This role diversification is cyclical. Feedback can be written or oral, but it is personal. I therefore have a simple test for the appropriateness of feedback I provide to student work: would I be pleased if we exchanged roles?

Scaffolding and Self-Monitoring Progress

SCAFFOLDING

The physical image associated with the word *scaffolding* is appropriate for a productive approach to advising. We construct a series of platforms close to a building under construction or parts of a building needing repair or strengthening, and we move it and eventually remove it as the structure begins to stand on its own. *Scaffolding* has a related and particular meaning in education: there are some things a student can do unassisted, some things she or he cannot yet do at all, and some things that can be accomplished with the help of a more knowledgeable person, a teacher or fellow student. This middle zone moves like North American football yardsticks as the team progresses along the field. The assistance provided in this middle zone is called scaffolding. The effective advisor (or any teacher) constantly reevaluates what the student can do alone, cannot yet do, and the progress, then adapts the scaffolding—helping students to get to a new level of performance or thought that they could not achieve without help, then building again from there.

Scaffolding works because it involves the student as an active partner in identifying what needs to be learned next. A student-centered advisory meeting should therefore begin with a three-part question to the student: where are you now, what is the next step, and what can I do to help you get to that next step?

I had a doctoral student who had drafted a paper based on her master's thesis. It was accepted by a journal, subject to moderately extensive revisions. The student decided to make the revisions but came to the conclusion that it involved a major reconstruction of the paper, and despite an eager beginning, the effort bogged down. When we met to discuss this paper after several months, I asked how the revision was progressing, and the answer was a fairly detailed set of notes but not much text. In short, a case of writer's block. I suggested that she write two or three sentences that she wanted to appear somewhere in the new version—a small goal rather than a big one. Then she asked if we could have a weekly writing time together for several weeks in a row so that she could benefit temporarily from an external support and the feeling of a deadline, plus some structure to the effort. A few weeks later she announced that she had accomplished more than we had set together as an objective. About a month later the manuscript was successfully resubmitted.

Sometimes students do not accurately judge the extent of the tasks they take on for themselves and it can become frightening. With this student my task shifted to giving feedback, as a stand-in editor, on the emerging complete text, and the student increasingly set her own specific writing targets. Progress was not steady; some weeks revealed none, usually due to competing obligations, but sometimes I suspect due to avoidance. The scaffolding I provided addressed both confidence and competence. It shifted in focus and moved with the student toward her desired outcome.

In direct teaching, the instructor chooses the content, the method, the timing, and the evaluation. In scaffolding, the teacher and the student build key elements of curriculum together. The image illustrates advising as a process of guidance and coaching strongly complemented by invitation, self-assessment, and self-regulation by the learner. Without those interim outcomes, advisors cannot effectively help students become independent contributors to scholarship.

STUDENTS SELF-MONITORING AND DOCUMENTING THEIR PROGRESS

If we advisors think of our task as scaffolding our students rather than directing them, we get an added benefit. The student role in scaffolded learning requires that, on an ongoing basis, graduate students consciously monitor their progress toward goals they play a part in setting, and they have a direct role in setting research and other goals to pursue. Giving students this explicit responsibility is a powerful learning and teaching technique.

What's more, many universities now formally monitor graduate students' progress toward their degree. Such monitoring usually takes the form of an annual or semiannual report of progress along the milestones of the degree, such as completing course or unit work, sitting for comprehensive or candidacy examinations, defending a research proposal, obtaining research-ethics board approval where relevant, collecting data, and so forth. At our university, these reports require a statement of the progress anticipated in the subsequent year. The student and advisor must both sign off on the evaluation of the past year and the plan for the year to come, because they are both accountable for achieving the goals set. These can be stated in broad terms, but students who do self-monitor, self-evaluate, and learn to set attainable goals in increasing chunks are not daunted by the accountability created by documenting their overall progress. Seeing a summary of their annual progress in writing, or illustrated in a portfolio, is generally motivating.

Students who do not make progress, rare (or not) as they may be, are reminded of the need to renegotiate their working plan, and the review then takes place twice in the following year. It may involve setting new dates for completion, avoiding time-consumers such as teaching assistantships, or stopping the clock with a leave of absence.

Some advisors may not like this evaluative part of their role. I have purposely proposed that this should be a responsibility shared by the student and the institution. The advisor's role should be limited to helping students achieve and document their progress (e.g., students welcome advisors' counsel on how to add publications under review or at other stages to their CVs, or having the advisor read over a draft annual report). Self-monitoring progress formally and systematically reduces or removes the risk of even the appearance of arbitrary imposition of expectations for a student, especially if the review of the progress reports is done in committee. For students doing well, it provides recognition expressed privately plus welcomed validation. For students not making satisfactory progress, it provides due process should a decision be required to impose a probationary status or even terminate a relationship, but above all it provides clear guidelines for the preferred outcome—improvement.

If documenting progress is not required by the university, department, or program, it can be instituted by an individual advisor, even rather informally. For example, in a conversation or (perhaps preferably) in writing, we can ask:

- What have been your major accomplishments in the last semester?
- What needs to be done next toward your degree?

- What kind of a schedule might be reasonable to accomplish that?
- When should we meet again to discuss whether the schedule is realistic?

These are not punitive questions; rather they are questions advisors ask themselves when updating their own lists of things to do, and they introduce their advisees to at least a modicum of time management tied to priorities. Advisors are modeling actions we eventually hope students will do on their own, and we can be explicit that this is our purpose.

3

MAINTAINING BOUNDARIES IN
ROUTINE INTERACTIONS

Graduate students need to be treated as educated, mature adults who have a contribution to make to scholarship and advanced learning by future generations. When they find their knowledge and skills undervalued, themselves in many ways dependent, and their contributions unrecognized, they are handicapped. Because the graduate-student "condition" contains barriers to mature-adult actions, advisors should hesitate to place the full burden for success on students' shoulders. Advisors' attention, care, and support are essential to graduate students' ability to live up to the mature-adult expectation. Being a role model in the discipline or profession is only part of the process. Equally important are the ways advisors generally conduct themselves in day-to-day interactions with graduate students—with mutual respect and good rapport. At the same time, advisors and students must be careful to observe boundaries between the personal and professional or academic domains.

Distinguishing Work and Home

PROFESSORS HAVE LIVES (USUALLY)

Separating home and work in students' minds and our own is part of student-centered advising. Advisors are typically highly devoted to their research and their graduate students. They also have lives beyond this dedication, with families, friends, hobbies, and other responsibilities. Advisees do not need to be intensely connected to the advisor's personal life to be successful, and in extreme situations inappropriate bonds can make the student, advisor, or family members vulnerable in the general sense of losing privacy, and also by expanding unnecessarily the perception of the extent of accountability. On the other hand, if a student has a legitimate reason to contact a professor at home (e.g., there is a problem in a laboratory animal facility), an exchange of names and greetings with whoever answers the phone facilitates communication.

There are two equally important principles here. First, professors' personal relationships need to be respected by students. Second, significant persons in an advisor's life need to know with whom the advisor works. The large amount of time, energy, thought, and emotion devoted to our students can become disrespectful of and threatening to loved ones if the two domains are not both reasonably integrated *and* compartmentalized. The purpose is to create comfortable but separate parts to our lives as advisors.

Occasionally entertaining student groups at home can build friendly links while maintaining clear limits of time and distance. The presence of our loved ones at conferences or at social and ceremonial events in the workplace reinforces the existence of our different domains of loyalties and reminds everyone of the need to foster them all in their place.

Some students and advisors and their families may indeed form viable friendships and other strong relationships. It is then crucial that other students who have for any reason a relatively arm's-length working connection are not made to feel that they are required to move into a closer relationship to get all the benefits of advising. So at the same time that I encourage connecting work and home (although I do wish I could bring less of it home on weekends), I emphasize the simultaneous importance of keeping them separate.

When students and advisors have established or clarified these zones of activity, it is easier for students to recognize that advisors have changing needs and may from time to time need more space or time, or a get-well card. Advisors too experience changes in their lives with the birth of children, marriage or divorce, changes in health status or deaths, caring for parents temporarily or in the long term, working for tenure or promotion, or receiving tempting job offers. Any of these can strain the relationship with advisees, because expectations need to adjust. If any such circumstance arises for you, tell graduate students that there will be delays or constraints to access, or there may be a need to arrange backup advising for a while. When an advisor accepts a new position at a different institution, the strain can be extreme. Professors often maintain advising at a distance but then need an on-site coadvisor. The student is typically expected to shop around. This is particularly hard on a student who has come to the advisor expecting to study with a particular expert, or who has convinced the advisor to facilitate a study that nobody else was attracted to. If a graduate student is not bound to a particular city, consideration can be given to funding completion of her or his studies at the new university.

In an extreme situation, a colleague died just before the start of my first semester as department chair. He had several doctoral students, and not only did they suffer concern for their degree and career success, but they also felt a deep personal loss. It was important to meet with these students, hear their concerns, and work with them to find new, mutually acceptable advisors who would not require them to start all over. Placing the full burden of finding new advisors on the stranded students would have overemphasized their adult status. Doing it together was a better way to treat them with respect as colleagues.

STUDENTS HAVE LIVES (USUALLY)

In addition to being responsive to changes in student needs, advisors should recognize the constantly strenuous lives of many graduate students. We do not need to know about our students' lives away from the university just for the sake of knowing; rather, the information is useful to help students succeed. This information includes whether they are living close to the edge financially and need to work nights or weekends to make ends meet, and whether they have families—especially young children or other dependents, or a partner who works shifts. Advisors are not required to personally know students' family members, but adult significant others should be welcome at appropriate social or ceremonial events.

Graduate students are mostly at an age at which having someone to love contributes greatly to their well-being, and they can be falling into and out of these relationships, with all the emotional consequences that entails. Some forge permanent relationships. Some bring, have, or adopt children, deal with aging parents or disabled siblings, and also face the prime period for the onset of their own emotional and mental challenges. They may have little time or money for social activities or to travel to visit loved ones or friends, and they may be living in less than desirable housing or eating less, or less nourishing, food than they need. Some leave families overseas and may have only fleeting opportunities for a visit home.

Treating students as emerging colleagues implies that advisors will respond positively to their students' requests for adjustments in the timing or nature of expectations and provide a kind word and a question about their health or happiness. Most universities have had students whose families were caught in the middle of civil unrest or natural disasters in their home country or region. Asking if they have made contact with their families, if they need to make a long-distance phone call, and if everyone is all right is not an intrusion. In fact, it is only right.

Maintaining Balance

Students sometimes run into trouble because they take on too many duties before fully realizing the extent of the burden of advanced coursework, reading and laboratory duties, grant and scholarship applications, the articles they commit themselves to writing, preparing for conferences, and more. Some if not most graduate students have for years been strategically planning, and sometimes changing, their academic trajectories through extra courses, volunteering, or other special elective activities. They now face a new array of teacher- and future-employer-pleasing possibilities that will have them burning the midnight oil well beyond reasonable limits. Students need guidance and permission in being selective about these additional undertakings, as attractive as every one of them might be on its own merits.

SELF-EXPECTATIONS

Our graduate students need help with setting realistic expectations for themselves, feeling empowered to say no to others and to their advisors, and extricating themselves from situations of overload. There are more than enough student cases of mononucleosis in universities. Another issue is whether our students should be getting all this required help from advisors or from others, such as more advanced students or, if they exist, workshops organized by student services or graduate student associations on campus and at conferences.

There is not a single magic script to accomplish this. One way to address issues of overload is simply to raise them in a public conversation, such as a seminar or research-group meeting, so that nobody feels personally criticized. I have had students make a large number of commitments and meet few if any of the largely self-imposed deadlines. There are often a few months of avoiding the question of when an article might be drafted, but eventually a conversation must be started.

I worked with an enthusiastic, knowledgeable, and well-intentioned graduate student who eagerly volunteered to help with conference papers as well as making sense out of an old data set that needed extensive work. He made good progress, fortunately, in his degree studies, and he did publish some other articles and presentations. After about a year with no word on the additional material, I asked him to stop by for a conversation. I told him how much his willingness to collaborate and contribute to collective goals was appreciated, how good he was at assisting with complicated analyses, yet I wondered aloud if perhaps he felt he had taken on too much at the moment and was just unable in a twenty-four-hour day to get around to the two projects on which there was no progress. I asked whether he still felt strongly committed to those papers or would feel relieved if I found someone else to help with them. I was explicit that I understand how responsibilities pile up, and that I would not hold it against him in any way if he let go, but I was also amenable to his keeping the dossiers, in which case, could we discuss a reasonable time frame for at least beginning the work? I was handing him an escape script in case he did not know how or was too embarrassed to compose one himself. I could sense his relaxation as he said he was indeed overloaded and appreciated being able to return these commitments to me without ill effect. We then discussed the general problem of graduate students' taking on too much and that it was a good idea to check in with one's advisor before accepting major commitments external to the prime responsibilities of completing the degree.

I could have said, "I'm taking these projects back from you because you have not made any progress for a year." Doing so would not have taught him how to deal effectively with such situations, and because there is a strong chance he will be a professor in the future, instead of learning how to administer punishment, he was coached in how to enhance his own future students' progress. Psychologists also know something else about punishment: It does not teach what it seems it should. Penalizing a student for taking on too much does not teach him or her not to take on too much. Punishment reliably predicts one thing: avoidance. Penalties teach students to avoid situations in which they will be punished, such as conversations with their advisors; thus it decreases the likelihood of a productive conversation about balancing the load. Students who take on too much are already punishing themselves. We do not want them to refrain from taking on any extra responsibility. Rather, we want them to pause and make good judgments about how much they can take on and deliver in a reasonable time.

DECLINING GRACEFULLY

Students therefore need to learn the ways to say no, or to take something under consideration and come back later with an answer. A conversation with an advisor can help validate whatever is the student's predisposition about the extra task. The advisor can remind him or her to weigh the advantages and disadvantages and especially to set priorities: what other commitment can be delayed or cancelled in order to do this new task, and where does it rank in the list of active commitments? It is hard for a student to say no; it is easier to say, "I'd like to think about that, and would it be all right if I got back to you on Tuesday?" or "I am interested in that project—may we discuss whether this is a good time for me to get involved?"

Graduate students need examples of good scripts to help them withstand internal and external pressures to load themselves up with commitments that they cannot complete in a reasonable time frame. If these model scripts come from their advisors, they will be more comfortable practicing them, and we can gently remind them.

Cultural Sensitivity

We in academia tread a delicate balance between "when in Rome, do as the Romans do" and extolling the openness and welcoming communities we hope we live in. The reality a "non-Roman" experiences on arrival is likely somewhere in between, but I have learned that it is surprisingly easy to make someone feel uncomfortable, even innocently.

GREETING

Students from some cultures—even adults many years our senior—need explicit permission to use informal forms of address. Recently arrived from the Middle East, a much more experienced teacher than I sat in my office as far back from me as he could comfortably adjust his chair. He addressed me as "doctor" and kept this up for many months after he was admitted to a master's program. He even did so when other younger students used my first name, as is our custom, and I invited him privately to do so. I still do not fully understand why this happened, but I think he felt that our role and status difference in the institution demanded his formality as a courtesy, and he was much less concerned than I, perhaps, that Western graduate students young enough to be my offspring or his were simultaneously using my given name. The point is that he was persistent in doing what he thought was right and proper. In retrospect, professors do the same; for example, first names are not normally used in university senate meetings. After he graduated and stopped by informally one day, I asked whether he would now be comfortable changing our mutual form of address, and with a smile he agreed. Were he not my elder, I know he would have still preferred an asymmetrical relationship, but the circumstances were now changed.

The best way to create a comfort zone is to discuss it, for example: "I usually use first names with graduate students, and if you are comfortable doing so, I would welcome it." Then be content with whatever the student does in the future, until there is an appropriate moment in which relationships shift, such as after a thesis defense or graduation.

When we meet new people, we typically shake hands whether they are men or women. But men need not be offended when a woman with her head covered (this may not be apparent with a wig) holds back her hand. There are happy occasions when we might pat a colleague or student on the back. If a handshake is a source of discomfort, such contact will be as well. The solution is to ask: "Are you comfortable shaking hands?" This creates a recognition that warms a relationship. And if you err, just smile and carry on with a very brief "Oh, sorry." Of course the same is true in reverse. If you meet someone who does not offer a handshake, don't take it personally.

COMMUNICATIONS

The aim of an advisor is to make all of one's students feel valued and comfortable enough to get their work done, which can be tricky when there are differences in sex, age, cultural background, religion, race, or mother tongue, just to name a few.

Some students speak and understand the language of instruction well enough to write a fellowship application but not to understand a joke. That does not mean advisors should not tell jokes, but a private explanation later is often very welcome, because what is funny might not at all come across that way in

a listener's second or third language. Being left out of a joke is
a form of social exclusion.

Expectations about normal classroom discourse also vary.
One day a student from Asia who had lived many years in Can-
ada and was extremely fluent in English was observing one of
my undergraduate classes. He had been reading about inquiry-
based learning and knew that classrooms could look different, but he was astounded that during my ninety-minute class
I addressed the whole class for only twenty minutes or so. A
hundred education students in an amphitheater were working
in pairs and small teams with material they and I had brought,
applying psychological principles to teaching plans for their
specialty subjects. He had never experienced this kind of classroom activity before and did not believe it could lead to effective learning. So I let him look at the many excellent essays
that I had just finished grading. I felt comfortable pushing
him to move out of his space into mine. I would not do that
immediately with students still suffering culture shock, but I
would welcome them to come and see how things can be different from what they were used to and to discuss it with me.
A doctoral student of one of my colleagues studied the experiences of Chinese graduate students at Western universities:
their biggest shock was not the language but the fact that they
had to decide for themselves a lot of what they would learn.

Cultural differences of one sort or another affect many
relationships between advisors and students. Some of these
are small and easily navigated, such as to whom one does not
wish "Merry Christmas," who does not drink alcohol or shake
hands across sexes except with close family, and who is comfortable with first names. Some are harder to manage, such
as deferential behavior when initiative is appropriate, or the

opposite. Advisors have superior status in the dyad and therefore need to initiate adjustments. Directly ask what creates the most comfortable zone with each of your students, and invite them to help understand these situations better. At the same time, welcome each student over time to come as far into the customs of the group as she or he is comfortable doing. Actions speak loudly in all languages.

Socializing at Home

Nearly every semester for over three decades, my wife and I have invited my advisees and their partners or guests to our home for a relaxed buffet supper and a few hours of conversation. These social events typically include other professors with whom I work most closely and their advisees, and the venue eventually began to rotate around the professors' homes. Students on their own created the tradition that these are jacket-and-tie occasions, which I have found helps to set a very pleasant tone. From the graduate students' point of view, these events help cement friendly relations with others who have similar interests, and they contribute significantly to their happiness.

Entertaining students at home is a wonderful way for family members and students to put names with faces, but there are some rules to observe. When I was department chair, a casual and positive comment from a student revealed that a wonderful young professor had his graduate students over one weekend evening. On this occasion most students drifted out between ten o'clock and midnight, but one remained somewhat longer, happily engaged in conversation. I heard no indication of any indiscretion, but I stopped by the professor's

door, closed it, explained some of the risks, and offered my
advice as follows:

- Never be alone in your home with one student for more
  than a few minutes—for example, for a student to drop
  off or pick up some materials. Plan any extended meeting
  in your office or a public place, preferably on campus; if
  it must be at home, ensure that there is at least one other
  person present.
- Every invitation given to students should indicate when
  a party starts and when it ends. If anyone tends to linger,
  thank him or her for coming and mention that you need
  to clean up and get up early the next morning. If he or
  she offers to help, say with thanks that you have a clean-
  up routine and no help is needed, as you walk toward the
  door. The end time is more critical than the start time.
- Always have a cohost. If you have a spouse or significant
  other, that is the person the students should meet. Otherwise, invite a friend or relative or colleague. The pessimis-
  tic reason is to have a witness. The optimistic reason is
  that we spend a large proportion of our waking hours with
  our students, we invest in them intellectually and emotionally, and therefore persons close to us need to know
  that they rather than our students remain in first place.
- Whether or not to serve alcohol is a judgment call. I work
  in a jurisdiction in which a glass of wine or a beer is a normal social courtesy, and the legal drinking age is eighteen.
  We offer wine and nonalcoholic beverages at our parties.
  However, when we entertain groups of undergraduate
  students we do not offer any alcoholic beverages, because
  some of them are below the age of majority and because
  my colleagues and I have a different kind of relationship

with undergraduates. From time to time a small number of undergraduates who volunteer on our projects have been invited to parties with graduate students. If in doubt about a student's age, ask—if he or she is a minor, offer nonalcoholic beverages, and explain why. If alcohol is not served in your home, you keep kosher or halal, or there is a food allergy, alert your student guests to not bring any food or drink in that category—they are not always well versed in these matters and welcome the advice.

- In general, do not privately employ your students to work in your home doing food service, domestic, or academic work, unless because of your university position you live in a house with an obvious public area intended for ceremonies and receptions and you hire students (emphasis on the plural) to assist. Although this is not by itself entertaining, periods of work are almost certainly going to be accompanied by conversations that we would not have with professional cleaners or kitchen staff. The problem is not the payment; rather, the challenge is being alone at home with a student.

- Make clear whether or not children are welcome at social events. One new student, a single mother from overseas with a young child, was torn between the strongly perceived obligation to attend such an occasion and the nature of the gathering. She had not established a babysitting connection and was concerned that her child did not yet speak any English and might not behave well. Fortunately she sent me an e-mail explaining her dilemma. I suggested that she might come for a while with her child and could feel completely comfortable leaving early, but if she preferred to stay home we understood her concerns as a mom, and these events were not in any way compulsory.

She chose to come with her child, and they left before the others with a paper plate of goodies for a treat at home. A student's sense of obligation also needs to be addressed sensitively. From this incident I learned to mention the above suggestions to students with young children, single or not, when term parties are announced. It is also perfectly fine to state in an invitation that adults only are invited.

After each successful dissertation defense, my wife and I also invite the PhD graduate and his or her partner or guest out for a celebratory supper at our expense, and the invitation has never been refused. Dinner out is an extension of entertaining at home. Similar guidelines apply; unlike a working lunch in a public campus location, an off-campus dinner for just two could be perceived a personal rather than professional event, even when it is not.

Socializing in Academic Settings

Socializing with role models is a valued part of the entry into a new world of scholars and advanced professionals. However, if not navigated with care, it carries risks to reputations and to the rest of the relationship between each student and the advisor and relationships among students. Graduate students welcome opportunities to enter the inner circle of academic life. The center of that circle is located, of course, at the university.

SOCIALIZING AROUND THE UNIVERSITY

I include on- and nearby off-campus locations in this category. Having an occasional working lunch together, or just a snack, can provide excellent stimulus to good conversation and creative thinking. If this takes place in public, say at the graduate students' center or a campus café, I see no problems. Visible on-campus locations do not give any hint of seeking privacy. Consider telling the department secretary where you are going, with whom, to discuss what, and when you will be back. When going to any less public venue—for example, the faculty dining room or an off-campus café or restaurant—I have asked other advisees or a faculty colleague such as a committee member to make the group at least a trio. It does not matter who rounds out the group.

And it is especially valuable to remember the word *occasional.* Infrequent get-togethers are quite different from weekly or otherwise regular gatherings for a coffee or beer. Of course the latter are not problematic if they involve all or most of an adult group of colleagues. The misperception my advice addresses is that an advisor and an advisee might be perceived as a romantic couple rather than professional collaborators. If they *are* a couple, that is addressed later in this chapter.

SOCIALIZING AT CONFERENCES

My students and I, and sometimes my wife as well, have attended conferences together. These occasions are highly empowering for students, and they are fun too. But there are boundaries, and failure to know and respect these boundaries presents reputational risks.

Our graduate students should meet the people whose work they read, perhaps also their students, and feel like colleagues. But conferences are among the most potent rumor and gossip mills ever invented. Work or other duties might preclude a

significant other from coming with us, and sometimes we may
be attending with just one accompanying graduate student.
There are several ways to make this a productive and pleasur-
able, risk-free event for everyone, and new professors especially
need to be aware of these considerations:

- Book separate hotel rooms. I have specifically asked hotels for rooms that do not have interior connections and
  even that they be on separate floors—I once did this at the
  check-in desk with three female students at my side when
  the hotel workers had assumed that colleagues would wish
  to be housed near each other. A possible and rare exception to this separation is the situation in which the professor has a significant other who knows the student very
  well, and the student sharing the room is of the same sex
  as the professor. Given how quickly conference hotels can
  book up, be sure to reserve early and to insist at the time
  of booking on rooms with separate beds. Given the role
  of appearances in fueling rumors, sexual orientation probably does not make a difference to this advice. Another
  exception might be a larger group traveling together (see
  below). Best of all is to get clearly separated rooms, not
  putting oneself or another in a situation in which the perception of unequal power or authority—whether the result of position, sex, gender, or age—becomes a challenge
  to a positive and productive relationship, and a possible
  source of real or imagined compromise to the professional
  relationship.
- Do not spend time in students' rooms. Do not let them
  spend time in yours. A hotel room is an extension of one's
  home. The lobby is the place to meet for any reason.

- When going out for a meal, include some colleagues or other students. An extended group event is more relaxed and a better networking opportunity for graduate students.
- Some conferences have late-night parties or receptions. Arriving at these together and introducing students to colleagues is very acceptable, but do not linger late at events that are clearly intended for students. If some faculty colleagues and friends are there, spend most of your time with them. Your students will feel much more comfortable.

In my own experience another situation has arisen. Four female graduate students and I had papers accepted at an international conference. My wife came as a tourist, although she knew many of the people at the association. She also knew all the students, and they knew her, from events at our home and at the university. Renting a nearby condominium time-share that accommodated six people was considerably cheaper than getting three double rooms at the conference hotel, and offered opportunities for shared times together during a couple of extra days before and after the conference. I found a unit with an en-suite bedroom for my wife and me, a second bedroom, and a living room, with total accommodation for six and a separate full washroom of which the students had exclusive use. I would never make such accommodation arrangements when traveling alone with students. In this case, however, I was well chaperoned, there were six of us, and we dined, went sightseeing, and attended the conference together. We took full advantage of these unique circumstances and happily showed our photographs of the trip to everyone at a seminar on return.

Physical Contact

IN THE UNIVERSITY CONTEXT

In the zone between handshakes and intimate relations, it is sometimes necessary in the educational setting for an advisor to touch a student. Examples include some coaching by faculty members in the performing arts, such as teaching arm, hand, leg, or back position, to guide movement and check for inappropriate tension—until the learner has mastered self-regulation; a guiding hand for using dental and other surgical instruments; and the touch a physical-education instructor might employ while teaching gymnastics. Sometimes contact is more general and coincidental, such as when several people stand closely together in an elevator, move heavy objects at an archaeology field site, or launch a boat. In some cases the physical contact occurs during university safety simulations.

The critical first step is not to presume that we as advisors have an unfettered right to make physical contact with a student. It might be an obligation, but the obligation extends to explaining to the student that some contact will be needed—this is best done in a group if possible. I do not intend the advice offered here to be alarming; it involves a courtesy that makes advisory relationships more comfortable to navigate. The explanation should include clear descriptions of what physical contact will be made and why. Then ask if anyone has any general questions, and also invite anyone who has a personal concern about physical contact to speak privately with you. In some cases it might be reasonable to have a graduate assistant or another student serve as an intermediary.

It is probably a good idea to ensure that published material, on paper or on the web, about a program or course in which there is necessary physical contact addresses these issues so that students do not choose programs in which they will not be able to benefit fully from instruction that includes sanctioned, professionally relevant, physical contact.

When contact is actually going to happen, avoid surprising the student; give a signal such as "I am going to guide your hand so you can feel the edge," then ask, "OK?" The "OK?" is largely rhetorical but is also respectful. If the student hesitates or says no, ask if he or she will be ready in a minute; you can work with someone else first, perhaps while the hesitant student watches. If necessary, meet privately and review the points made in preparation for this part of the learning experience.

The university context includes any place in which we represent the university, for example, a field site or a conference. I have met and advised students who naturally initiate a hand on a forearm, a clasped handshake, an arm on a shoulder or on an upper back, and who are eager to lean forward and conduct a conversation a nose-length away. These gestures can be reciprocated on an occasional basis. Generally, let the student define the comfort zone. In one case a student with whom I had been discussing the possibility of advising over several weeks responded to my agreeing by leaping up and giving me a happy hug. Our normal greeting afterward remained a smile and "How are you today?"

I also have met and advised students who feel cornered in moderate proximity of any sort, physical or verbal. It does not matter whether we or they are male or female. In some cases the students change over time and become more relaxed. Because of differences in real and perceived authority, it is the advisor's responsibility to gauge the space needed by each student, not theirs to gauge ours. Some students have even changed advisors because they felt intimidated by the lack of regard for this space, and I am not talking about professors who crossed any serious boundary. The professors were being their usual warm, friendly, caring selves. Some students prefer to be welcomed more slowly or more formally into the inner circle.

ON THE FRINGE OF THE UNIVERSITY CONTEXT

My university is in Quebec, and a greeting or farewell that includes a gentle embrace and a kiss on each cheek between men and women and between women is common and normal. Men also often hug. However, precisely because the peck on the cheek is normal in some social contexts, this is a greeting between social equals or nearly equals. It is not the appropriate norm in dealing with one's students, especially at the outset.

For advisor-student relationships, arm's length is the default for physical contact. Although some students arriving at a party or reception might want to give you a hug, doing so could make others uncomfortable, especially newer students. A warm verbal greeting by name (never "dear" or any other term of endearment) with a handshake is the best greeting for all. Sometimes the students with a closer sense of connection may time themselves to be the last ones out. That allows a more personal send-off.

In general, even after months or years have passed, a student who has preferred a more formal level of physical contact might still prefer a handshake to a pat on the back, a hand on the arm, or another common greeting. Wait for a signal initiated by the student or former student before asking whether she or he welcomes or minds being greeted otherwise. For example, one student in a group conversation made a point of saying how she had become comfortable after two years with the local kiss on the cheeks and closer personal distance. Still, let the student take the initiative. If one student initiates a hug and another new student stands there, offer a handshake and perhaps comment that the first student has been around a long time, or something to that effect. Handle gaffes with an apology and good humor. The best comment might be "I'm so glad you came!" That, a normal handshake, and a warm smile will be remembered positively.

Hard News

One of the hardest tasks is communicating dissatisfaction with anything from the standard of work to punctuality, reliability, treatment of other students or colleagues, contributions to a collective effort, or professionalism. Another is intervening when we suspect the advisee is experiencing psychological distress. Performance and personal issues are sometimes separate, but either can be the cause or the trigger for the other, and rarely do these problems end or improve without intervention.

There are some simple practical steps we can take to minimize the discomfort of these situations. First, aim for more privacy than usual. Delivering one of these messages constitutes one of the rare events for which a fully or almost totally closed office door is appropriate. Generally, the office door should never be fully closed when one is meeting with a student—just enough to muffle sound. Second, advisors should have a box of facial tissues located where a student can reach one without asking, and that box should always be present, not only as a signal of bad news. Third, make extra time for this conversation; these messages can cause physical discomfort, tears, blushing, and ruined makeup. You want to be able to invite a distressed student to wait, regain composure, and leave when the path to the nearest washroom is likely clear of familiar faces. Redirect your attention to your e-mail, or talk about the future—whichever is more appropriate. Allowing the student to save face shows continuing care for her or him.

Despite a long conversation with me in the winter about these sorts of issues, a master's student started to noticeably underperform in the spring. I discovered incomplete required-course units. A pupil file was missing from a school following data collection. It had been picked up with the student's notes inadvertently, but such a confidential item should have been returned instantly, not set aside to be delivered on the next planned trip to the school. Preparation for presentations and articles was typically done at the last minute, long after cocontributors were ready. And more. Although the thesis was progressing adequately, I was investing a disproportionate amount of time to maintain this relationship. I asked the student to come in for a meeting, and said, "I need to discuss something very important with you. I value your creativity and our comfortable relationship. But I am uneasy with some of the things you have done in the past few months and am having trouble imagining three or four more years of working together with this discomfort." (Several months earlier I had similarly met with her, pointed out that her continuing in the degree absolutely depended on her remaining current with her work and maintaining positive relationships with field sites, and received assurances that there would be no recurrence of such incidents.) I spelled out the accumulated list of old and new incidents and announced that I must withdraw my letter of support for admission to the PhD program and the offer to advise in a doctorate. I enumerated the conditions under which I might reconsider and reassured the student that I would actively ensure successful completion of the MA in the interim. On this second occasion, I also suggested that the student's career ambitions would be well served by related professional experience before pursuit of a PhD and that I would provide employment but not academic references. The tears flowed and the tissues were used. I was again promised action. The student successfully applied for and obtained a relevant job, and finished the MA thesis—submitting it within minutes of closing time on the last possible day. The conditions for resuming a PhD application were never met, and the student has taken an alternative career direction. This second and more difficult conversation took place six months before the PhD would have started—a last-minute announcement would have been very unfair.

Sometimes behavior change is possible. When I was department chair, a faculty member was subjected after class, within earshot of other students, to rather negative comments by a master's student about her fashion choices. One of my advisees explained the observing students' discomfort to me. I undertook to speak with the offending student, whom I knew casually as a very pleasant and intelligent young woman. I thanked her for coming in, told her how pleased instructors were with her academic work (I had checked), but also that I had a sensitive matter to discuss. I do not remember the exact words that followed, but they were close to this: "This is not an academic matter. It is more about professionalism and courtesy, and it is therefore also a bit uncomfortable for me to discuss this with you. It has come to my attention, and I am sure that you understand I cannot tell you how or from whom, that on at least one occasion you have made remarks to Professor X about such topics as fashion choices. I am sure you meant no harm, but I think you crossed a couple of boundaries that you should not have crossed. First, such advice is the reserve of close friends, family, and sometimes employers. Second, such matters should always be addressed in private. You should not have commented in the way you did. Have I missed anything relevant about what I was told, or was this not the case? If it did happen, I would appreciate having your assurance that you will not do this sort of thing again." The tissue box was again called into action. The student then gathered her composure and said she just realized that she had done this before and nobody had ever done her the favor of providing direct feedback. She apologized to me and went directly and apologized to the instructor, and the incident was history. Except that she came to me a few months later (her master's advisor was leaving the university) to ask if I would be her PhD advisor; we agreed, and it was a delightful relationship.

Another challenging situation is communicating with a student who is in a personal, health, or academic crisis. The first impulse is to ignore it because our primary responsibility is the work, not personal well-being. But I do not believe these can be separated in a student-centered relationship, which, I repeat not too apologetically, is the most beneficial for both student and advisor. The words I have used are more or less these: "I sense that it has been hard for you to keep up lately. We have had to delay meetings, and some things we both hoped would be taken care of are not started. I know you don't like being in this situation, but I have a feeling that something external is interfering with your productivity." Sometimes the student comments at this point. I then add, with pauses, "Do you think it would be a good idea to take advantage of the confidential counseling services we have on campus? Would you like me to dial the number for you to make an appointment?—I could leave the room while you speak. Would you be more comfortable if I walked down with you to make an appointment in person?" Never once has a student I worked with pushed back and refused any help. Students may get time-management assistance or be referred for medical, mental health, or financial aid. They might mask their challenges, but when prompted by someone they trust, they usually welcome a guiding hand. They might fear punishment. I am always clear that their seeking help is for our mutual benefit, and any knowledge I obtain in this interaction is private.

Occasionally students have a predilection for telling us too much about their personal lives. When relevant, it is still useful to state that we have noticed that the student's progress or availability is not at a satisfactory level, but I would not ask for details. It is sufficient to state that we do not want to be more involved in personal matters, but we should, in a meeting with preset starting and ending times, look together at progress toward agreed goals and adjust them if necessary.

Advisors are not usually experts in solving student crises, so it is best to contact counseling, an ombuds office, or a similar student service where professional help or a referral is available. Advisees appreciate advisors' standing with them as they try to appeal grades, recover from missed deadlines, deal with poor performance in a required course, cope with a temporary impediment, or begin to address what could be a challenging personal problem. We don't, however, want to find ourselves in over our heads regarding advisees' personal lives.

I usually phone or e-mail a student I have not heard from
for a few weeks. Students see this reaching out as a remarkable
expression of support. Advisors are nearly always strong advo-
cates for their students, but sometimes students need help in
choosing to steer a healthy and productive path. Arm's length
is not far.

Life Coaching

One of my students conducted workshops at our teaching-
improvement service, but I had never directly observed her
doing so. On several warm days she appeared at our meetings with an exposed midriff. I do not normally comment on
students' appearance, but our relationship was close and relaxed, so out of the earshot of others I asked, "That's a very
nice belly, but might it distract some instructors, and will they
take seriously what you say about teaching?" She replied that
she dresses conservatively when she gives a workshop. I responded, "Are workshops the only place on campus you meet
these professors?"

"Oh, I had not thought of that," she acknowledged, and
we cheerfully continued to discuss her research.

The necessity for some clothing items such as protective
laboratory coats, hard hats, or goggles is easy to address, but
it is also vital to prepare or coach students that how they dress
and speak matters at conferences and presentations, during ac-
creditation site visits, when we have guest speakers, or when
they are going for interviews. Some business schools require
professional attire at all times, and when I attended teachers'
college we had the same requirement. Although most pub-
licly funded schools have relaxed teachers' and students' dress

codes, many have not, and most have probably not relaxed to the point of exposed bellies.

How students present themselves affects the authority others perceive in them and, eventually, how they perceive themselves. I almost never wear a necktie or jacket to work, but I do when visiting a school, making a presentation, or speaking with a donor. When my students and I do these things together, dress matters. Life coaching begins with addressing such small items in a friendly manner as they come up in context, not by giving orders or being overly prescriptive. However, we need to be very clear to make any such intervention only when it is germane to our functions in the institution. In most situations, what our students wear is their business, so our advice should be constrained by our specific knowledge and scholarly or professional goals.

Some life skills that my students and I have addressed together include writing a curriculum vitae and preparing for interviews. Not only advisors but also senior students have the expertise to succeed comfortably in these situations. Student associations and career centers on campus sometimes offer workshops. I have also shared model CVs and done informal mock interviews with students, and as a group they have supported each other with even more intensive simulations.

The real test in life coaching, however, comes with issues that are larger, sometimes very personal, and almost entirely off limits. Advisors and students often have much in common, but the most common difference is generational (eventually, if not at the beginning of our career). Culture, sex, religion, personality, and lifestyle differences can make advice that has worked well for us irrelevant or worse for them. A good basic rule is not to give advice that is too direct or too personal,

but to feel comfortable sharing some personal experiences if
the student asks how we navigated a particular path, explicitly adding, "But what worked for me might not be best for
you—it just illustrates that we can deal with these issues cre-
atively, each in our own way." Graduate students, especially
the ones who are moving toward a friendship relationship with
their advisor, are quite likely to visit or call us for life advice on
a number of matters. When the topic is whether or not to consider a job offer somewhere, that is a fair topic. When the issue
is whether or not to marry a particular individual, have a baby,
or break up a relationship, I begin by saying, "That's a tough
one. I feel honored that you care about my opinion, but you
are now asking about areas well outside my expertise." Then
my advice is always that they may wish to consider speaking
with a professional such as a counselor.

Advisors should certainly never take sides, even inadvertently—for example, by remarking that having a baby might
delay degree completion for a female graduate student. I have
had students who were never slowed down at all by having ba-
bies, and others who were, both men and women. It is fair to
remind students that graduate schools usually do allow them
to stop the clock with a maternity, paternity, or adoption leave,
to ask whether or not the student contemplates such a leave,
and to discuss expectations for what should be accomplished
toward a dissertation while on leave—the acceptable default
being nothing.

Students have asked if I could recommend a good personal
banker or realtor; questions like these are answered easily. At
the other extreme, one student literally walked out of a very
long relationship and broke down in my office, stating that
she did not know where she would stay that night. I phoned

my wife and confirmed that our guest room was available as a backup. Meanwhile, the student made a better arrangement with a fellow student. A couple of years later she wanted us to meet her new beau. It was a lovely wedding!

One of my doctoral graduates spoke at a regional meeting of an undergraduate honor society. Her presentation, about the positive impact of goal setting on student performance, led many in the audience to ask her afterward if she would be their personal life coach. She did not take any of them on as clients, but this does point to a conversation that we can and probably should have with our students: what are some of their life goals, especially regarding their career, and how we can possibly be of assistance to them? When they have difficulty, ask about goals; this helps them focus on their own best path to achieve them.

As advisors we should focus on helping students define or identify their own life skills, but we can share from time to time when we have relevant expertise and guide them toward help. And if we can't give good advice, better to give none: Bad advice can create tension, chip away at a good relationship, and undermine your authority as an advisor. One final suggestion: if you have an advising or seminar group, consider having general conversations about life-skill topics the students propose, not about one student's crisis. Perhaps invite a guest from the career or counseling service.

4

QUAGMIRES AND STICKY SITUATIONS

Universities are creative, inventive learning places, but they can be minefields of drama, mystery, and intrigue. And sex. These are not issues that can merely disrupt an advisory relationship. They can potentially destroy it, along with reputations, health, careers, and families. I could start each section with "Do not . . . ," but even my advice here is sometimes nuanced. The best general advice, then, is to be aware that at some point you will have to handle at least one of the following situations.

Advisor versus Advisor

Some colleagues will be close friends, with others we will maintain comfortable working relationships, and there may be discomfort working with some others. The reasons do not matter much. Our students should never be drawn into discomfort or disputes between advisors. Students must navigate among us in courses, for administrative reasons, and because their friends are advised by our colleagues.

When my students ask about selecting a course taught by a

colleague with whom I have a substantial disagreement, or just minimal contact, I encourage them to pursue their interests. When students ask about inviting a colleague with whom I am uncomfortable to be a member of an advisory committee, or to be nominated as an internal reader of a comprehensive examination or thesis, I might reply that I have not had a lot of experience interacting with the suggested person in this role. In this situation you might say, "I prefer to work with colleagues with whom I share more in common regarding content or approach," and then suggest others. What you should not say is "I don't like him or his work."

As a former department chair, I have had access to privileged information about teaching and supervision, and the confidentiality of such information must be respected. At the same time, I am very aware that students talk among each other, and rare is a professor without a reputation. I cannot contribute to such conversations; rather, without pointing to any individual, I say, "It would be unprofessional and perhaps illegal for me to comment on that, but let's look at a longer list of potential committee members [or whatever] and make a list of people with whom we would both be happy to work."

Another challenging situation is competition for students. This can happen at admission, when students are assigned to advisors or choose advisors, or when someone is approaching a stressful career-evaluation point such as a promotion and realizes that the advisory file is a bit thin. In one extreme and inexcusable case that came to my attention, a graduate student told his advisor that another professor was trying to get him to switch to him as advisor but he did not want to. Students are not commodities, and it is extremely demeaning to treat them as tick marks in a promotion file. It is also a serious affront to one's colleagues. This behavior cannot be resolved entirely between advisor and student. First, reassure the student that you greatly value having him or her as your student, but that the student needs to decide in the first instance where his or her interests are best served. If that is with a new advisor, then there is no rule against changing. Second, because the initiative came from the potential new advisor and not the student—a situation that I consider inappropriate—ask the chair or program director to handle it. It may not involve an actual dispute between the advisors, but it could result in one.

Students change advisors even when there is no improper recruiting. Over four decades, I have had two switch to other advisors in the middle of their doctorates, whereas two came the other way, and a few switched to me from other advisors between their master's and doctorate. Those who left did so because they discovered that some of the foci in my research were not of great interest to them. They each continued working on their core topic with another colleague, and they invited me to stay on their doctoral committee. I did. In one case, the intended new advisor also came over to discuss this. In both cases, putting the student's interests first was key, and no collegial relationships were challenged.

The students whom I took over came from different conditions. In one case the advisor had died—this required a compromise on my part, because the student was well advanced in data collection. Fortunately our interests overlapped, we forged a very positive relationship, and she was able to finish the project with new insights. In the second case, the department chair asked if I would take over a student who had burned bridges with two previous advisors. A very caring master's advisor initiated one change because she perceived a better match of working styles. A second, initiated by the student, was the result of a perceived need for more personal space. A third arose with support from the master's advisor but was initiated by the student, who felt that student-student competition had soured her supervisory experience with her advisor.

In all the advising changes I have observed, it was possible to avoid professor-professor conflict, but equally, each could tempt such conflict. Although in each situation the bulk of the responsibility for successful advising rests with the two key players, it helps if the administrative unit discusses change-of-advisor policy and procedures from time to time, states explicitly in its student handbook that this can be done, and outlines steps that should be taken when it is contemplated. It is most helpful when the student and ex-advisor have remained on friendly terms and both initiate the change. More often, however, the situation is uncomfortable, in which case the receiving advisor must ask whether the student has discussed the situation with the current advisor; if not, then with the student's consent the two professors could talk. In one case, I had to insist that the student take the uncomfortable step of telling the current advisor. We anticipated correctly that he would feel hurt, probably because he had not perceived the student's discomfort in their professionally productive relationship. I reiterated to the student that my colleague and I had an active working relationship and friendship, that a condition of taking on the doctoral advising after she finished her MA was that the student needed to do her part to preserve the link, and that it would in the future benefit all three of us. This might seem to be a contradiction to the earlier point about not involving students in our disputes, but it was the opposite. With our discussion of the relationships, which included equipping the student with some of the things to say, anticipating the response, and preparing for how to deal with it, she was educated and empowered to make a tough decision and help preserve a valued relationship. It taught her that relationships outside the primary advisor-student dyad are important, too.

Finally, relationships among advisors can be tested by administrative actions. For example, a program director might say to an advisor with a large number of advisees that she or he should consider not taking on a particular student because someone else, perhaps early in a career, does not have "enough" students. This is delicate, because the more senior among us should care about our newer colleagues, But when students do some of the choosing, and especially when they have sought a particular advisor, the intervention can prompt negative feelings. There is probably no one best solution, but starting with the premise that the student's interests must come first, a coadvising arrangement may offer promise. The student and the initially approached advisor should have some say in the process.

Refugees and Wanderers

Refugees is an irreverent term for students who are stranded without an advisor, or might soon find themselves in this situation. Most tragically, the advisor may have died or become incapacitated. Sometimes an advisor takes a new position and completes the advising of advanced students but newer students are sent looking for new advisors. In other situations, students and advisors decide to part ways, or the student is very uncomfortable and seeks a new arrangement before discussing it with the current advisor. Most universities do not allow doctoral students to be without an advisor at any time after

the supervisory connection is established, so program directors and chairs commonly assign or take on interim advising while an ongoing relationship is sought. The process resembles the search for advising by a new applicant when this is the regime, but it imposes serious and time-sensitive pressures on both the student and potential new advisors.

For students, these pressures and fears can include mourning or grief, lowered self-efficacy, uncertainty about financial support—especially from research grants—impact on time to completion, and worry about how the new and perhaps rapidly undertaken interpersonal relationship will work. Sometimes students who had formed a cohesive group are scattered, and collaborative projects risk disruption. Faculty members are usually asked to take on additional advisory loads without any further diminishment of other parts of their workload. Yet I have never found professors to be unsympathetic to the needs of stranded students, unless perhaps we are dealing with students who claim to be escaping an unhappy advisory relationship.

But stick-to-itiveness is sometimes valued too highly by advisees. Students seeking release from an unsatisfactory advisory relationship should talk with their program director and receive help finding a new advisor. The director and student can create a list of the most appropriate people to contact—thereby limiting the nomadic period—and the reception by potential new advisors may be better if the program director makes a few phone calls or leans on a few door frames to briefly explain the circumstances and clear the path for a sympathetic hearing. Sympathy is more forthcoming when the student is stranded through events beyond his or her control rather than by a choice to leave an advisor. Whatever the circumstance, I still recommend to students that they meet with the program administrator, perhaps as a group in the case of death or medical emergency, and plan new possibilities together. A phone call from the program director or chair to say that a student is being referred can help open doors.

When I was asked to take on a doctoral student whose relationships with two previous advisors had broken down, I was undoubtedly prejudiced by this information. It was necessary to remember that just a part of the total information was provided and that I did not need to know it all. But I had a large advising load and a full-time administrative position at the time, and I did not know the student well. I discussed the strategy I would take with the program director, then met with the student. After she described her research proposal, I stated that I would let her continue with the project, but until our relationship had developed its own trust level, I needed her to agree to an initial period of 100 percent compliance with regard to the collection and analysis of the data, writing and editing the dissertation, dealing with administrative tasks such as annual reports, and meeting mutually agreed-upon deadlines. Another breakup could have led to the student's being "withdrawn" from the program. The student worked hard and communicated the barriers she felt she faced—and we addressed these together, our relationship warmed, the need for dictatorial rule faded, and she went on to an academic career. When it is warranted, set firm guidelines with explanations, but remain open to a good outcome.

Wanderers are a subcategory of refugees, a group of students who for any reason have not yet connected or been connected with an advisor. They may be just starting, they may be in a program in which they need to find or be assigned a supervisor after some common program requirements are completed, or they may be newly stranded. To all the other difficulties faced by advisory refugees, they add rather aimless wandering from door to door asking whether someone will advise them, and they often take too long to make a decision. Other labels I have heard for these students are *lost souls* and *strays*. In the worst-case scenario, they go from office to office until they hear what they want to hear or they get any expression of interest at all.

The program director or program committee should be advised of the existence of wanderers, because they are wasting a lot of their own time and experiencing needless anxiety, and too many "exploratory" meetings are not a fair expectation of busy faculty members. I usually ask wanderers about their interests and with whom they are talking. If that list is longer than two or three people, I tell them that they should narrow their list to a smaller number before we discuss advising. I do this because usually they have not invested enough time and thought in focusing their research interests around work that is going on in the department, but I am willing to help them identify who the appropriate people might be if they can articulate their interests clearly. If they are totally stumped, they should talk first to the program director and to other students, and perhaps with a personal or career counselor on campus, before they knock on any more faculty doors.

Another form of wanderers is fortunately rare but very visible. These are students who take what appears to be forever to complete their degree requirements and who work their way through multiple advisors over many years, making a very little bit of progress with each, then somehow get onto another professor's list on the occasion of an advisor's sabbatical or medical leave or moving to another university. Some are friendly and charming, never having had a major difficulty with an advisor, simply staying off the radar. The successive new advisors seldom know or check the past history. These students cannot let go of the hope of eventually obtaining a doctorate, but they carry on without making a scholarly contribution anywhere, but also without causing trouble. These students consume a lot of advisors' energy with little mutual benefit. Some have learning disabilities or emotional problems, topics addressed elsewhere in this book. If and when they ever finish a dissertation, often after several changes of topic, the supervisor will have had invested more direct and frequent input than normal.

It is very difficult for an individual supervisor alone to resolve the situation of the long-term wanderer. The key is program- or institutional-level intervention—not necessarily a guillotine, but at least short-term contracted goals and deadlines that, if not met, result in withdrawal or dismissal from the program sooner rather than later. And any action must respect the local procedures for assigning supervision—students may need to be reminded to follow these guidelines and to refer to the appropriate policy on paper or the website. If your program does not have written policies about changing advisors, it is time to form a drafting committee.

Sometimes refugees or wanderers may complain about feeling "owned" or bossed around, and sometimes they cite more serious matters such as verbal abuse, unfulfilled financial promises, sexual pressure, or worse. More often, though, they have lost interest in the subject matter or feel unsupported in their efforts. Except for refocusing the student's interests, it is a bad idea for advisors to try to manage these situations alone. Students should be redirected to recognized dispute-resolution processes in the department and institution. Help them make the phone call if necessary, but getting involved in what might be a one-sided perception, without the authority of position to do so, is an invitation to ruining colleagueship.

Advisors also need to keep in mind that we ourselves, not someone else, may be the problem. Excessive unrewarded demands, repeated feedback with a negative tone, reaching too far into personal space, unjustifiably favoring one student with a larger stipend or more authorship opportunities—or the opposite, reprimanding one student based on hearsay from another: these and other advisory misbehaviors do exist. We need to reflect from time to time on how we interact with students and ask whether the refugees or wanderers are perhaps our creations.

Conflict and Rivalry among Advisees

Even in advisory and program cohorts, in which students most often form strong and mutually supportive bonds of friendship and colleagueship, rivalry may rear its ugly head. Here is an example from where I work. One of our most prestigious national fellowship programs requires departments to rank the applicants. Survivors are ranked again at the university level, and finally a national jury reviews the short lists. It is not unusual for one's advisees to be in direct competition with each other, let alone with others in their cohort. They know that although I will have worked to help them build their CVs and write their applications, I may be asked to rank my own nominees. I never share my rankings with the students. All students need to be reassured of the esteem in which they are held by those closest to them, and reminded that eventually they will be successful. But they must persevere and keep in mind also that there are unpredictable elements in all such competitions. It hurts when one student gets five rejection letters in a year and another gets a six-figure multiyear fellowship on the first try.

Students compete in other ways, too, even if it is not evident to them. For example, some race to finish quickly, others rack up presentations and publications, they are assigned better or worse study spaces or offices, and they get different class grades. Some rivalries reflect personality differences. I knew a student who had apparently become good friends with a fellow advisee. The second student, it turned out, started complaining to their advisor that the first student was not fully cooperating or otherwise contributing. The advisor took the side of the complainer, reprimanded the accused student, and actually encouraged the first student to find a new advisor for the doctoral part of the program. The accused student did not feel empowered to challenge the accusations and welcomed the invitation to find a new advisor. Soon after the student made a new advisory arrangement, however, the former advisor realized that the stories were not true, candidly regretted influencing the student to seek a new path, and provided many superlative reference letters thereafter. The ending is not always so reconciliatory. One of the worst examples I ever witnessed involved a student who accused another of contaminating biological culture samples and set up a webcam to try to record the evidence.

Advisors need to be careful not to fuel rivalries between students. If we are in a position to be providing funding or other resources to students, there should be a defensible minimum, and we should be sharing or publishing the policies so everyone knows why differences might exist where they do. We should support all our students in building their publication record so that they stand out in major competitions. My own advisees and I make a list of prospective projects and possible timelines. I make a point of highlighting their successes, not only to encourage and celebrate the student who has earned the praise but also to remind other students that this oppor- tunity—like many others—was there for all. And even when some students are delayed, we continue to pursue the goal. I had a student with a recurring health problem. A paper ac- cepted subject to revision took over a year to revise, but we persisted, meeting sometimes weekly to get it done. That stu- dent got more time. Another student has more publications. Others went to more conferences. These opportunities were set out with reasonable equity, and the process is discussed collaboratively and regularly. Differences in final outcomes for each student are not perceived by the students as the result of favoritism. The rivalry is also minimized, when possible, by students doing some things together.

In some disciplines, especially in the humanities, students may be working on their own or be in smaller working groups. The variation I have described may not exist simultaneously among several students but, rather, sequentially over time. Usu- ally students will still compare themselves to previous, more se- nior students, those newly admitted, or even some who have graduated. It is usually easiest to at least briefly mention these different kinds of experiences very early in the supervision pro- cess, and not merely invoke them when a problem exists and when they might sound like rationalization rather than prin- cipled choices.

The core challenge for advisors is to set common goals, with variations as needed in the means to achieve them. Stu- dents understand that different circumstances bring them to- gether. Some have family responsibilities, others have part-time

jobs they may not want to relinquish, others have virtually unlimited financial support from their parents, and others overcome physical or other disabilities. Some are quiet and laid
back, and others thrive on competition. Often they are from
different countries, have different cultures, or speak different
languages.

One of my goals at the outset with all my students is that
they obtain major financial support from a prestigious external
source, if they are eligible to apply (some sources are closed to
foreign students). It is clear that this will not happen in every
case or the same way, but they are all treated as though it were
possible. When I get an invitation to write a book chapter, or
when I am planning a book of contributed chapters, for example, I find that this is an excellent project in which to involve
students. The authorship model can vary from solo to joint,
or the student or students as lead authors. This opportunity
is distributed among students. This certainly spreads out the
writing workload, and it also shifts the emphasis away from
competition among students. When we write grants, students
are always a part of the process, especially if they will benefit,
and we sometimes create working subgroups for specific grant
projects. We try to publish parts of all dissertations. The same
care is provided in engaging students in conference presentations, lunch with a visitor, and other academic perks.

If advisors are fair and seen to be fair, our students will
learn both by example and by the clear articulation of the principles by which we organize our scholarly, research, or laboratory work and interact with our students and colleagues. In
an advisory environment that minimizes interstudent rivalry,
it is easier to recruit volunteers to help with writing, organizing a seminar, collecting data, or anything else. Not all competition is bad: The context is critical, especially a context in

which one's advisees are equitably supported in their efforts to succeed. Then when one student steps forward, others do not worry that they will not also get a similar opportunity. Rivalry and competition in an environment perceived to be unfair, or that arises from uncontrollable problems such as personality or previous bad experiences, leads to dysfunction. Students might, as a result, drop out, develop lingering doubts about their self-worth, and make bad decisions about careers and relationships.

Procrastination and Delays

We all do it. All right, *I* do it. And the terrible thing is that sometimes when I wait to the last minute to do something, it comes out well. Even more reinforcing, I sometimes discover close to the deadline that the obligation was canceled. Such outcomes reward exactly the wrong behavior.

Students procrastinate. It may be the number-one complaint advisors make, although that might just be a lament that students postpone our priorities in order to address their own. Unfortunately, students are not as proficient at cranking out last-minute masterpieces. Efficient performance of complex tasks is partly the result of extensive experience and practice with good feedback along the way.

Many academic responsibilities are complex or a grind. This applies to the work of advisors and in many ways also to that of students. Whether it is grading essays, completing travel requisitions, or editing thesis drafts that we find tiresome, other, more rapidly rewarded tasks easily push ahead in the queue.

However, sometimes procrastination has other close associates. One of the nastiest is perfectionism. After all, smart people (of course referring to our students) have gotten this far by doing things nitpickingly well. The essence of perfectionism is failure to recognize when a piece of work is good enough, as good as it can be at a very high level without the neglect of every other obligation. The distinction between perfect and a high state of "good enough" can be elusive. One student, an award-winning professional, worked with me, then with a close colleague, finished a complete doctoral dissertation draft, delayed and delayed making the small remaining corrections, then died unexpectedly before submitting the thesis. More commonly, students have been forced to withdraw because they have overstayed time limitations or the realities of life overtook their academic ambitions.

Combating perfectionism is not easy. There is a limit to what advisors can do, especially if they themselves are perfectionists. We can provide positive models. We can say, "Don't do as I do." Ideally we should not procrastinate, but within the realm of the possible and the likely, it is more helpful to emphasize with all our students, individually and in groups, that no product is ever perfect. Seldom do contributions to the knowledge base remain state-of-the-art forever, and rarely is a thesis totally devoid of grammar or other minor mistakes. I repeat to my students that every time I look at my decades-old dissertation with penciled corrections on many pages, I find a new error. (Of course I don't look at it too often!) Students and advisors might from time to time write articles, proposals, chapters, grants, or scholarship applications in close collaboration. The collaboration can range from coaching to coauthorship. Advisors can offer advice on a student's own text or discuss examples from published work or anonymous texts received for review. This is a good time to discuss the format required for the submission, and the differences in presentation between a thesis, a journal article, and a conference presentation or a poster.

Regarding the student's own work, I discuss the criteria for deciding when the item is ready and how this is usually accomplished in several steps. I highlight that with an article or thesis, the goal is not just our total satisfaction but also to meet the standards or criteria set by the journal editor, conference selection committee, or external examiner. In these and many other situations the student will have a chance to fine-tune or make minor corrections to the product later if it is accepted. For articles, it is common wisdom that a request for revisions is more likely than immediate acceptance.

Sometimes perfectionism can be the result of deep-seated insecurity rooted in past experiences with never-satisfied parents, teachers, or other close adults, or low self-esteem that cannot be overcome by the mere kindness and good efforts of an advisor. Professional help may be needed. The student needs to be encouraged or convinced to visit the counseling or other service on campus, or to join a self-help group that a student group has organized. It may be necessary to offer to pick up the phone, or to suggest that a friend be recruited to accompany the student in making and keeping an appointment.

Also core to perfectionism is setting unrealistic, unattainable goals. Advisors are the source of many of these goals, but students bring a good supply of their own. Students typically underestimate the time and effort needed to achieve their goals. Modeling the making of realistic estimates is part of what we try to share in the normal process of doing our own research and in our research training. But we also need to notice when students stop communicating with us, look haggard, or hold

back tears when we ask about their progress. I find it very helpful in such situations to say that perhaps the student has hit a
brick wall, and together we can figure out how to get past it.
What is the number-one priority that must be accomplished?
We set this as the first goal to attain in solving the problem.
The problem to be overcome might be part of our joint en-
deavor, but it might also be a class assignment or a home issue. Without getting into the realm of private matters, I ask
what would be the very next small step to achieving that goal
and when time will be available to make that one small step.
I then say, "Let's set that as the first deadline," and also set up
a later backup deadline if necessary. I urge students to call or
e-mail me for congratulations when they accomplish that or
even make a good effort. It does not always work, but it can
snowball into success.

Perfectionism is a bad habit. It is maladaptive. It sets people
up for disappointment and lower levels of productivity than
they might otherwise enjoy. Only well-supported, directed,
and deliberate practice can chip away at it.

Not every delay is a result of procrastination. Students deal
with waves of assignment overload, suffer from their inade-
quate time management, fight fatigue, are hijacked by custody
battles over young children, endure physical and mental illness
as well as skiing fractures. Or parents visit from out of town
and stay longer than expected, the first trimester of an as-yet
unpublicized pregnancy is spent in continual nausea, and the
unexpected car, house, or computer repair requires extra working hours—most likely bartending.

Advisors should not demand progress on research or writing under such circumstances. It is fair to point out to the
student that a project is running late (remember the box of

facial tissues when posing such questions), but ask whether any unusual difficulties have come up, and provide a face-saving exit. Ask if there is anything you can do to help move the project along, and if it would help to reconsider together the next steps and set a reasonable timetable. If there is a real deadline, and especially if the task is very challenging (such as extensive reworking of a rejected journal article), it might be wise to offer time to work together in planning or actually do-ing the task.

Overall, a student-centered advisor should be engaged to some degree in guiding or coaching his or her student's writ-ing for journals or book chapters or conferences, and should have discussions about this work without necessarily assuming that the work is jointly conducted or jointly authored—that will vary according to the context.

Disclosures

This is a matter of distinguishing between the wish and the need to know. I once had agreed to work with a collegial, enthusi-astic, and brilliant graduate student, but for several months I remained slightly frustrated with her draft thesis ideas. Then the student disclosed a learning disability whose nature we were able to partly circumnavigate, and the output zoomed. Behind the scenes, the student constructed an elaborate sup-port system to help keep her on task and on time. Productivity nevertheless had its ups and downs. Our working relationship benefited from my being informed about the student's situa-tion, but I did not thereby earn the right to pass on that infor-mation. When it came time to apply for scholarships, we had to discuss again whether or not to make a further disclosure.

The student made the brave move to turn disadvantage to advantage and allowed me to mention that the achievements to date had been reached in spite of this hurdle. The rewards came, but I will never know whether the openness mattered or not. It was, however, more than a strategic decision. It was an important acceptance of identity and an invitation for me as advisor to join in resetting deadline expectations and a flow of productivity that maximized success for the student and also for our ability to work well with each other.

Advisors need to know about any issues that might impede the quality of the work and that require us to adapt. We do not need to know about issues that the student is successfully mitigating elsewhere, for example, through a student-disability, counseling, or health service. Some things are none of our business unless the student wishes to change that. A trusting relationship that may need time to evolve is essential to deciding how much disclosure is warranted. The student must always be given the space to be in control of what personal, private information is disclosed.

The previous example of learning disabilities is not the only circumstance in which disclosure might become an issue. There are many parallel situations. Students may not wish to divulge information about sexual orientation, income, marital or other relationship status, life-affecting health issues, or other very personal matters that may or not affect the many tasks to be accomplished by a graduate student. Some of these types of information are more likely to be shared than others. A student stated forcefully on one occasion that even an oblique comment about medication was an exceptionally personal one, clearly putting up a warning not to go there, but much later the same student volunteered that a change in medication was causing an interruption in meeting deadlines. Both statements were fair.

Sometimes departments or programs ask students to write autobiographical statements as part of an application process to graduate studies, and these are seen by many members who serve on an admissions committee. These essays are a serious challenge for students with extreme personal histories. The instructions need to state clearly that they are not being asked for disclosure of matters they consider private. These essays should be explicitly about their public lives. However, sometimes they reveal something about mentors who inspired them, about escapes from war zones, floods, or hurricanes, or about their medical histories. It is hard to keep some personal information, such as physical disabilities, private. I also remember a mature applicant who had a gap of several years on his CV, and the committee speculated about what might have happened then. He could have been hospitalized, in prison, traveling the world, or anything else; we quickly realized that in our discussion we were going beyond our right to know. All that mattered was whether or not the information we had at hand was verifiable and sufficient to make an admissions decision.

Personal statements are also sometimes explored in interviews of short-listed applicants. Great care is needed not to push students into corners on matters that we do not need to know.

Need-to-know is a difficult concept. There are programs in which the role of highly personal information is contentious. I am not taking sides in these issues, just describing the situations. In one example, directors of a dental school wanted to restrict the clinical activities of students with hepatitis. Those responsible for a medical or dental school might care about

HIV-positive status students in surgery, if only to take extra care. Directors of an education school might consider requiring criminal police checks on students because school districts require them for employability. These are matters that should be addressed and argued at the institutional level, where legal and ethical advice can be applied to the whole category of activities.

Personal statements and interviews can be very ad hoc. In these interactions with prospective students it is not a good idea for us as advisors to force disclosure. Those in other roles, such as ombudsperson or department chair, may have legal or other obligations to address. The advisor should not be asked to act as the proxy on behalf of these officials, first because it distorts the advisory relationship, and second because whatever legal protections a university might offer to such officeholders are not likely to extend to an individual research advisor in that capacity.

Some matters related to disclosure seem much less serious. One of my students had considerable experience as a text editor but did not want to be expected up front or assigned to engage in more of such work, so chose to strategically omit it from the CV. It is the student's choice to put such talents on the table later or not at all.

A student who is protecting personal information when the advisor does not need to be privy to it is in a vulnerable situation. That creates enough anxiety without added pressure from the advisor. Similarly, advisors who are made aware of personal information become vulnerable and need to take extreme care to preserve confidentiality as long as the student wishes. I know of an incident in which a student and an advisor met by chance at an off-campus counseling clinic—as it turned out, to see different professionals about unrelated matters. The student dropped by the advisor's office a few days later, having decided that it was helpful to tell the advisor that a family matter was being explored. The advisor reciprocated with similar general information, thereby leveling the playing field. The student's problem later mushroomed and impeded progress in research and writing; as a result of the chance encounter, it was easier for the advisee to come to the office again and say, "Remember when we met . . . ?" and then reach for the box of tissues. In general, the advisor's role is to listen respectfully, ask how he or she can help, ask who else in their shared circle is aware of the information. Help the student be in charge.

Conflicts of Interest

People are in a conflict of interest when information or relationships they hold in relation to positions of authority might be to their own or another person's private advantage or disadvantage. A simple example is accepting a gift from a student, and especially doing so privately. A bottle of wine or a cake brought to a party does not create a conflict of interest. Neither does an infrequent small book or a few cookies with a thank-you note, or a souvenir bookmark from a holiday.

On the other hand, if one student makes a repeated habit of bringing even small gifts, it is appropriate to decline early in the sequence and explain that the generosity is deeply appreciated but this is not appropriate. Being invited to a student's home for dinner (as long as there are not just the two of you present) is not a conflict, but being invited out to a restaurant is. Offers of use of a vacation home, travel on a private aircraft

owned by a parent (this temptation was once dangled when I
was dean of students, but it could have occurred in an advisory
context), or a free shopping trip to an establishment owned by
a student's family all constitute conflicts of interest. In some
places in the world, these courtesies might be seen as directly
parallel to the private fees collected by teachers and coaches
who have no salary or whose salaries do not pay the rent, but
they are still likely to be serious conflicts in all situations. If it is
essential to supplement earnings, it should never be with one's
own students, anywhere. It is a conflict of interest to provide
paid supplementary tutoring to one's own students or probably to any from the same institution. There is no solution to
these conflicts other than to decline to become involved. After
graduation is different.

One of my advisees was the wife of a professor in the same
program. It is a small program, and there are not multiple
sections of the classes. When she needed to enroll in a class
taught by her husband, we arranged for a third party to conduct all the evaluations. Even having another professor grading the work potentially creates conflicts of interest that are
sometimes difficult to avoid. The other professor could have
been on the tenure committee for the teaching husband. As
advisor, I had to separate some of my interactions with the two
parts of the couple. The husband and I shared grants; these
funds could not be used to support this graduate student, or
it would have constituted nepotism, a specific case of conflict
of interest. That created a disadvantage for the student, one
that bothered me because it contradicted my commitment to
try to create comparable financial situations for all my students. Avoiding conflict of interest takes priority, however. It
is also not to any student's benefit to be perceived by others as

having any unfair advantage through other connections to an advisor. Failing to respect the university's conflict-of-interest regulations and principles can also have serious disciplinary or legal consequences for the student or advisor—for example, in the case of inappropriately using government-funded research money.

Other conflicts of interest can occur in advising. These include agreeing to advise a relative or the friend of a family member, or someone related to a person from whom you receive income, for example, for consulting or for serving on a board of directors. Another conflict can arise if you are asked to promote the application of someone who is connected through family, friendship, or business. If the applicant is known personally, then it is acceptable to write a letter of recommendation, but it must begin, as should any such letter, with a declaration of the relationship between the writer and the student being recommended. A vote or oral statement given at an admissions committee must be prefaced with a declaration. A special and more serious conflict of interest, addressed separately in the next section, occurs when a romantic relationship arises between an advisor and an advisee.

There are situations that feel as though they are conflicts of interest, but they are not. Advisors write letters on behalf of their students. When you are nominated for a teaching or advising award, on the other hand, letters may be required from students. As noted in the later discussion of reference letters, a colleague or another student should normally solicit these letters. A typical student response is delight at being able to return one's compliments. The process is public, the relationships among the parties are explicit, and there is no expectation of compensation.

The primary protective shield against conflicts of interest is to immediately declare them to your administrative superior—certainly in writing if the institutional rules require it, and at least follow up an oral discussion with a confidential memo (not sent by e-mail). Then take the steps needed to mitigate their negative effects. In many jurisdictions, a conflict exists only if it is hidden. Once declared, it is no longer a conflict as such, as long as the mitigating steps are then taken. One example of a mitigating effect could be to arrange for coadvising or to step aside totally, but the latter might disadvantage a student who has sought you out for particular expertise. Totally stepping aside is the only acceptable solution in extreme cases such as an intimate relationship. Another could be to take a secondary role such as committee membership rather than direct advising. At the heart of all these options is making the process public and accountable.

In many areas of research, advisors are required to have procedures certified by a research ethics board. But we are normally left to monitor and mitigate our own conflicts of interest. Conflicts can arise innocently. How they are dealt with, quickly, honestly, and deliberately, is an integral part of how advisors convey the importance of integrity to their students.

Sex

ADVISOR AND ADVISEES

No.

Universities and research institutes are communities of adults who share educational and other common interests. Because student-centered graduate education means nurturing future colleagues, it lowers barriers that formality and distance sometimes provide. Advising is primarily one to one, fostering close interactions. Not surprisingly, amorous relationships arise. Nonetheless, advisors must not have sex with an advisee or any student for whom they have academic responsibilities. This applies equally to opposite- and same-sex relationships.

A few papers have proposed exceptions, for example, with students who are at a similar stage in life, perhaps established professionals who have returned to study. My response is "Sorry, no." I am also, of course, limiting this discussion to people who believe they are in a consensual relationship. If the relationship were not consensual, we would be discussing harassment, assault, or rape, issues that considerably exceed the current focus.

Mutual consent is not a valid justification. Major power differences remain within the university, and other professors are inhibited when evaluating the student's performance when they know that a student is in a relationship with a colleague— they may not want to offend the colleague with negative assessments of the student's work. A sexual relationship between an advisor and advisee is an extreme conflict of interest. Some professions—for example, associations of physicians, psychologists, and lawyers—revoke licenses of members who have had sex with a client or patient, even a former client or patient. Suppose there were a normal professional-client relationship, but years later they meet by chance and the hearts sing. Most associations still insist that the professional find sex elsewhere. Graduate students are not clients or patients, but there are parallels in terms of authority, disclosures, and dependencies.

Students sometimes initiate consensual sexual relationships with advisors. They should not. Advisors have a dual duty: do

not seek or initiate a sexual relationship with an advisee, and
do not accede to one. Keep your office door open. If the hall-
way is noisy or a conversation might be overheard or might
be disruptive to others, agree to keeping the door slightly ajar,
but open enough to see in and out. If the student closes it, ask
politely to keep it open. Do not delay to explain. If the student
makes advances, make it clear that there has been a misunder-
standing. Ask the student to leave your office. Go directly to
your administrative superior and report the incident; ask to
annul your advisory relationship with the student forthwith
and find him or her a new advisor. Then summarize the event
in a memo and give it to your chair or director.

I recall the case of a student who made such a sexual proposition to an advisor, having misinterpreted months of the advisor's collegial treatment as a unique personal favor. During a
private meeting, the advisor explained that there was no such
intention, because all students were given such opportunities;
the student felt shunned and jilted. Yet the student persisted in
the belief that there was a romantic opportunity. This was an
unusual case of a student who was emotionally quite unstable,
but that made the case even more difficult to resolve. The advisor immediately informed the department chair and arranged
for someone else to take over responsibility for the student,
but the student persistently phoned the advisor's home. The
ex-advisor had to get an unlisted telephone number and eventually filed a harassment case against the student within the
university and the legal system. The student was dismissed.

It sometimes happens that a sexual liaison is not explicitly
proposed but appears to have been offered. It might be as overt
as "I'll do anything to get an A on that paper!" or something
the advisor interprets as a possible proposition, be it words,
body language, or a touch. Usually, ignoring such language

and keeping the discussion serious and academically focused works. If not, the correct response is something like "This conversation is not going in an appropriate direction. Our work together must be 100 percent on a professional basis. Let's reschedule the rest of this discussion." And do so. Then announce a need to do something down the hall, leave the office, and ask the student to leave as well. How to handle the next meeting will be hard to predict; I would begin by acting as though the incident never occurred and, in a friendly but businesslike way, getting right to work. If the student wants to apologize or comment briefly, listen courteously, accept any apology graciously, and get down to work. In such a situation in which ambiguous signals could be misinterpreted, I would not necessarily end the advisory relationship. But I urge that the incident be shared with any significant other and that future meetings with the advisee be conducted with a fully open door. No recurrence should be allowed.

Advisors must also not even appear to have crossed this line. Do not hang out with one student in cozy retreats around campus, or date surreptitiously. Do not have a graduate student record the greeting on your home, mobile, or office voicemail. Do not give your house key to a graduate student, unless she or he is temporarily house-sitting when you are away. The risk of suspicion is compounded by the small but real possibility that a student later could become mentally or emotionally unstable (we are discussing, overall, the age group at which such onset, even if rare, most often happens, and it was the case in the above example of the student who felt jilted), seek retribution, and even start a false rumor or formally prosecute a case of sexual assault. At stake is your reputation as someone who does not violate a trust, whose office and home are safe places, and who values his or her job, career, and integrity.

ADVISORS AND OTHER GRADUATE STUDENTS

Each university community defines this limitation according
to local values. Some campuses totally forbid any sexual relationships between faculty and graduate students. Few, if any,
condone them. If the student is in a different department, the
introduction is unlikely to have come from local academic contact, so this situation calls only for care not to place each other
in conflict of interest—sometimes examiners are selected from
other departments for examinations, faculty scholarships, or
promotions. In such cases, disclose and recuse, and then treat
the relationship as if it were external to the university. If the
relationship existed before one party became a student or a
faculty member, follow your university's conflict-of-interest
guidelines.

ATTRACTION TO A STUDENT

Attraction is an understandable feeling in a community of
adults, but tread carefully. Respect your institution's rules.
These rules exist because, as obvious as the boundaries here
might appear to some readers, the line has been crossed in the
past. In general, find love elsewhere. With the student, conduct yourself as if there were no attraction and let the flutter
subside. If restraint is not assisted by friends or a counselor,
then withdraw from any academic relationship with the student and continue to resist. Doing so reflects respect and caring for the student.

Equality does not exist until after graduation, if ever, and
an amorous relationship would disrupt the apprenticeship.
There does not seem to be the same negativity about a re-

lationship between an advisor and a past student as there is about love between a professional and a former client. I am not advocating that an advisor should simply delay responding to attraction to a student until graduation day. However, connecting later may be different. Some professional associations do not impose a lifelong ban, but five or so years. This is an active ethical controversy. The best advice is probably to "have a life" outside the university. If that life is being built or rebuilt, use relatives, friendships, social clubs, sports, or professional or online dating services to connect to new loves. Except among other available faculty members, campus is not a suitable dating pool for advisors.

Pursuing a student is not the same as becoming attracted to someone whom you originally met off campus and discover later to be a student. That student is certainly not your advisee, so proceed in a way that does not create a conflict of interest for either of you. If a conflict is discovered later, declare and remove it. Again, do not offer to be the advisor, and do not hide the relationship or how it started.

5

CAREER SUPPORT

The major part of the relationship between advisor and student normally ends around the time the student graduates. Advisors move on in a renewed cycle of students and projects. Students get on with building their lives and careers. However, just as advising is introduced by an overture in the form of making the advisory connection, there is often an encore to be played. These are parts of student-centered advising that begin during active advising but sometimes continue for years after the student's graduation. Some of the value gained when advisors make these additional investments is instrumental: it helps our graduates obtain scholarships, postdoctoral fellowships, and jobs. Examples of ways to achieve these ends include forwarding notices of awards and positions, writing letters of support, and active networking at conferences. Some value, however, is intrinsic: It adds to students' self-efficacy, broadens their skill base, and adds to the feeling of being welcomed into the scholarly or professional circle.

Beyond the Fixed Curriculum

Among the career-related roles in which graduate research students can apprentice with their advisors to varying degrees,
formally or informally, are participating in conference presentations, teaching, presenting at departmental seminars or
brown-bag lunches, reviewing for journals or conferences, and
consulting. These opportunities vary according to the discipline, but they are all useful contributions to the total experience of student-centered advising. These are the kinds of
activities in which knowledge creators engage. Even if advisees
are not heading for an academic position, they enjoy these ex-
tensions of coursework and dissertations. Implementing them
requires a balancing act, especially not overloading them with
too many such responsibilities. They should be offered as opportunities with some degree of expectation. Following her
successful thesis defense, one student said to me that her advisor was a "slave driver" and the main lesson she learned was
how not to treat her own future graduate students. On one
hand, bringing students into central and even lead roles in our
own core work requires generosity on our part, but we need
to balance our expectations and create a workable, reasonable
plan. Nevertheless, emergencies happen (e.g., a last-minute request for major changes to a grant application), and we do
need all hands on deck. We need to ensure that there are recognized benefits, not necessarily cash, associated with these extended activities.

Students have different strengths and can support our efforts in different ways. The fact that one student is an excellent statistician does not mean that she or he should do all
the number crunching and never get a chance to help with a

workshop, literature review, or finding a home for an unpublished manuscript. Other students may have a weaker public presence and, without training and practice in a more private setting, should not be asked to present a research proposal to a committee. However, we must be careful not to always favor one of our students over others or make excessive demands on one just because he or she is competent. I try to share the anticipated opportunities for extra learning in either individual or group meetings with my advisees (the offer is important, not the format in which it is made) and then ask them to express interest, individually or in pairs or groups. Sometimes I reach out. "Freebie" help is acceptable when there is a mutually desirable quid pro quo.

One such role is presenting at conferences. This includes elements in which some students are not proficient. Most students at the graduate level have mastered the fundamentals of written communication, but they may be terrified of speaking before a large audience, and equally worried that the audience might be very small. My faculty colleagues and I send an e-mail to our students inviting them to gather informally or in a seminar to practice conference presentations and job-interview talks, with feedback from us. Sometimes only a few people are available, but any number can be helpful. We try to initiate student conference proposals with multiply authored presentations so that if a whole hour is assigned to an accepted presentation, individual students can present shorter chunks. If multiple authorship does not make sense in a particular discipline or case, the advisor can offer to help make the presentation, or propose the format as a round table or poster rather than formal presentation if the options are available, for less experienced students. Students (and some advisors) need to learn that slides need to be readable (no yellow print on an orange background) and letters large enough to be easily legible at the back of the room. They need to learn how to engage the audience in the presentation through an activity or meaningful questions, as well as how to use a microphone or to project their voice if one is not available. How many slides can you fit into twelve or twenty minutes? How long does it take to present the material on one typed double-spaced page? May I read my text or slides? How not to read your text aloud! How much text should go on a poster? What makes a good graphic? What do you do at a round-table presentation? It starts to sound like informally teaching our students how to teach, and, in fact, it is. There may be a relevant workshop on campus or online, but the content and the audience are more authentic when you help students prepare for real events. One unexpected lesson occurred at a local presentation. Two student presenters got caught in traffic and arrived barely on time. The lesson learned was to aim to be at a presentation site very early, not just early, just in case of traffic delays or a projector that does not work.

At conferences, one of the most valuable contributions is introducing students to the people who write the research they read. If there are social receptions, attend together and meet their students and colleagues as well.

Because graduates may want to teach, teaching skills can be acquired in graduate or undergraduate courses (as well as seminars or workshops offered by your university). Students can sit in on advisors' classes, help prepare a short activity related to their research or special interests, or look at student assignments from the perspective of the instructor. They could help develop rubrics to evaluate assignments. Advisees should not be asked to grade assignments unless they are formally employed to do so. One of my students, employed in another department as a teaching assistant, developed a research project around an assignment she created, and a journal article was her reward.

One activity that several of my advisees have valued was assisting with reviewing journal articles. Usually the opportunity is to help me with journals or conferences for which I review, but in a recent case one of my advisees—first author on an earlier manuscript—was invited on her own to review a paper on a related topic. On one trip to a conference, doing this together was a useful activity during an airport stopover. Several of us read the manuscript, compared notes, and drafted the evaluation. The journal editor agreed to list the students among the reviewers at the end of the volume.

About a year before one of our research grants expired, we began planning the next stage. Our students had been at the table throughout the process and were encouraged to make suggestions on any part of the application. In one successful application, a student proposed the central theme. Students are excellent editors precisely because some of the content is unfamiliar to them. It helps us to anticipate how a nonspecialist jury will respond to the text. Students can also assemble reference lists and update CVs as well as other parts of the presentation; we do not necessarily remunerate time spent in these activities, but participants (as opposed to onlookers) normally get priority for being funded if the application is successful.

My teaching assignment once included a group of professional master's students in a project, somewhat similar to a thesis, based on evidence-based practice in their work as educators, health workers, and other disciplines. Some of my doctoral advisees asked if they could gain experience advising master's students on these projects. In one year, when there were many projects, the department was able to create a second section. Three students became paid coinstructors, and I guided them through the process. The following year two students wanted to repeat the exercise; I could not arrange payment but did arrange formal appointments as "coinstructors," listable on a CV, so they worked with two or three students each. In a subsequent year, one of my doctoral students asked for some supervised volunteering experience advising master's research projects. I was eager to accept her contribution with one or two students but immediately consulted the department chair about how we could formally recognize the contribution in some nonmonetary way, given that cash and coinstructor status were no longer available as rewards. In the end, it was possible to recognize the contribution on the student's transcript by using an individual reading-course credit.

Other examples include bringing students along in consulting (one split the honorarium with me on an assignment to design a distance-education mastery test) and encouraging students to engage in governance in the department, a student association, or a research center. In some fields the development of a patent application can generate a student apprenticeship, whether or not the student is a part owner.

Involvement beyond the fixed curriculum adds professional skills to students' portfolios. It provides foundations for collegial and collaborative relationships to continue beyond graduation. It builds pride and confidence as graduation and employment near. Along the way, having learned to carefully edit draft papers or reports, for example, can also improve the first drafts of dissertations, saving us many hours at the end when deadlines loom. The investment can pay off for all parties.

Reference Letters

Reference letters are a critical part of the extended relationship between advisors and students. During the years of study, such letters support scholarships, field placements, and election to student offices. After graduation they are needed for postdocs, jobs, and awards.

My personal policy is, whenever this choice is possible, to write a very strong letter or decline to write one at all. In some situations students have no choice but to ask for a letter from their past advisor, at least during the first three to five years after graduating. Students do not need to maintain frequent contact with their advisor after graduation, but they should at least provide an updated CV and a short narrative when they need a reference letter, and after that time letters from more recent employers or colleagues are more relevant. If the relationship has continued beyond that point, letters can still be appropriate, but in the first paragraph they should summarize the advisory relationship and how it has continued.

Providing a positive and informative letter is rarely a problem with my advisees; it has been more commonly a problem for students who have simply been in one of my courses or for whom I was a thesis-committee member. When asked for a letter in the latter two cases, I sometimes have no choice but to reply that I do not feel I am the correct person to write a strong endorsement and that they should seek referees with whom they had exceptional success and a closer relationship. Over four decades, I have had only a few master's graduates for whom I was not comfortable recommending continuation to a doctorate, but I was willing to write a one-page letter in which I mentioned the positive qualities that I recognized, for example, honesty, collegiality, or specific successes. This was a deviation from my preferred choice of a strong letter or none, but sometimes students are really stuck and they require a letter from their advisor, even though I know that the recipient will probably read between the lines and detect the weak endorsement—and I am forthright with students about this risk. For students in either of those two situations, I stated in a private conversation that I would not write a letter in support of admission to a doctoral program, and it was up to the student to find other more positive endorsements. In the cases of the even smaller number of doctoral graduates about whom I could not in good conscience write an enthusiastic two-page reference letter, I have not said anything in particular directly. None of these, fortunately, sought an academic position, and I was less hesitant about writing a letter of support for a position in which loyalty and hard work—assuming they did exhibit these qualities, as they did—were more important than academic promise. Sometimes very good people make a wrong decision entering a doctoral program and they need help exiting graciously. When a letter has been absolutely required from me as former advisor, I have discussed the outline of the proposed letter with the student. Sometimes a shorter letter that addressed specific abilities or accomplishments met the need. None of these former students, that I am aware of, is unemployed. If I have not been in touch for a few years with a former student about whom I cannot write a strongly supportive letter, I usually decline, unless the required letter is simply a confirmation of our past connection. When I decline, I try to suggest other more appropriate sources of reference letters.

Those of us at the receiving end of these letters know there are no bad letters in a litigious world. When in doubt at the receiving end, phone. I remain astonished at the number of students, especially undergraduates, for whom I have agreed to provide a letter and whose new employers or graduate directors do not check the references. Any reference letter should make clear that a telephone follow-up would be welcome. This is not because I have anything negative to say—if I had, I would not have agreed to be listed—but all reference letters should normally be confirmed at the receiving end. But I digress. In short, there are great letters and there are very neutral, read-between-the lines letters that specify the students' strengths and silently hint at the weaknesses.

In my experience it can take several hours to create the first version of a letter for a student. The result is usually about two pages long, and it might extend to a third if I list specific publications or other noteworthy accomplishments. Mentioning work in progress is especially relevant early in a student's career, when the items are in preparation or under review and a reader cannot easily confirm the honesty of the CV without a reference letter backing it up. Many years ago I had the usually pleasant assignment of taking an applicant for a faculty position in my department to supper when the intended host became unavailable. I did not have a chance to read the CV until the next day. The CV indicated that a submitted manuscript had been accepted. Coincidentally, I had earlier reviewed a blind copy of that paper for a journal. I recognized the title and remembered that I had recommended rejection; the editor had agreed. We hired someone else. There is a lesson here: always check the details of a student's CV before creating a letter extolling its marvels. It is fortunate that journal editors commonly share decision letters with reviewers; this sharpens our reviewing skills, and it also can help keep job applicants honest.

A strong, honest reference letter describes how the advisor and advisee are connected; the students' collaborative and individual accomplishments, initiatives, interpersonal strengths, integrity, and contributions to the group or department; and the student's potential in relation to each of the specific criteria for the position or award. I always try to include an anecdote about how some success was achieved; this shows that I have personal knowledge of the student's performance, and my letter adds detail not available in the CV. I do ask students if there is something they especially want me to recount in the letter, but I do not ask them to write the letter for me. If the student has overcome a major hurdle in life and this is relevant to the letter, with her or his explicit permission and following a conversation about how it will be phrased, I include this privileged information. It might be about overcoming a disability, a life tragedy, or other challenges. Writing reference letters is an extension of the advisor's obligations as strong advocate for his or her students.

Once a base letter is drafted, creating future updated versions is usually fairly easy. Just take care to correctly change the student's or addressee's name, address, salutation, and any internal references to the positions or awards when building upon an older text. When writing several letters on behalf of the same student, I have sometimes forgotten to change the addressee or date and thus had to reprint many envelopes and letters. In this age of easily updated electronic files, always double-check before sealing the envelope or uploading the PDF.

A companion activity to writing reference letters is directly coaching students and recent graduates in their application letters and referring them to campus services that offer workshops on making applications. Students are not always sure what information to include or exclude. My typical practice is to ask them to sketch or outline their material independently; then we discuss an outline to develop the first full draft of the application, and I look over their drafts, including any that they draft at a workshop on or off campus. This level of engagement is not usually needed after the first effort or two.

Students and graduates may not know that it is permissible to telephone or otherwise contact a potential employer or other target audience with questions about the kinds of information they might be especially interested in receiving. Such contact, done professionally, might well be remembered when the application is on the table.

Students do not normally see reference letters we write for them. However, discussing the main points we propose to include, and possibly reading parts of a draft at a private meeting or on the phone, can help a graduate student learn about her or his strengths and areas for growth. Because we are usually very positive in such letters, students are sometimes surprised even to the point of mild embarrassment to learn that their advisor holds them in such esteem. It is much more comfortable for advisors to extend these compliments through an overview of the points to be included in a reference letter, or sharing a paragraph or two, than in a direct statement.

Although most jurisdictions treat reference letters as strictly confidential and students waive access, this is not universally the case. Some jurisdictions have totally flipped the situation. In the province of Quebec where I live and work, students and people in general have the legal right to see any letter written about them; if the letter is from another province, state, or country, they have the right to see that letter but without information about the author. A student cannot waive access. My personal practice is therefore to share a copy of the final letter as well—I realize that not everyone is comfortable with this, but it keeps me accountable, and it is also an extremely validating experience for students to be introduced to the world in a positive manner. There is no evidence that this has created a situation in which every letter is artificially glowing; it does likely prevent letter writers from being nasty.

When a glowing reference is not appropriate, there are ways to convey this message in your letter without being unnecessarily negative, especially as more and more letters are submitted online: for example, being brief (perhaps one free-form page or not filling all the available space on an electronic form), giving prominence to the invitation to phone for more information if desired, stressing the facts of what the student has done, and not emphasizing potential to excel in future work. These signal constraint in the recommendation without being negative. The times that I have had to take this approach have actually worked well. I think students usually know their limitations. So we can say forthrightly that we are not comfortable making an enthusiastic recommendation but will comment on the student's strengths and accomplishments. If the latter are too few, the student should likely have been counseled out of the program long before, and refusal to write a letter at all might be suitable. Most potential advisors and admissions personnel can sniff out an ambiguous or noncommittal tone in a reference letter.

Developing letters with students gives them a model for letter writing as the tables turn and they find themselves supporting the recognition of their own future advisees. An advisor who is uncomfortable about, or otherwise prevented from, sharing a reference letter with students can, for instance, use

the main text of past letters with the names and details of locations deleted to illustrate how a very strong letter is constructed. To maintain distance, these can be letters about
undergraduates. But it is important to at least outline the kinds
of topics you like to include in a strong reference letter so the
student can help you by providing an updated CV or excerpts
from his or her CV and transcripts, annual progress reports, or
other sources. Furthermore, no matter the disciplinary norms or
legal framework, graduate students are sometimes asked to write
letters for undergraduates or others, and advisors should offer
them advice and guidance. At the very least, advisors should
share anonymous model letters and offer to read drafts. In all
cases, jurisdictional, departmental, and disciplinary norms need
to be respected.

There is a flip side to the reference-letter coin. If you happen to be nominated for teaching or supervision awards, letters will be required from your students. Sometimes professors
need letters from students for jobs or academic promotions. As
I mentioned earlier, requests for student letters should come
from a nominator other than the professor herself or himself;
advisors want to avoid the perception that a positive letter
written for a student must be reciprocated.

The main point is that graduate students need to learn
from their advisors the ins and outs of writing and deciphering
recommendation letters.

Publishing Together

Jointly publishing with students is extremely common in the
sciences and some social sciences, and much less common, but
not totally absent, in the humanities. As with group advising,
addressed earlier, this is probably related to traditions in the

disciplines. The individual scholar can still thrive in the humanities and arts, although some funding agencies are making this harder, and it is difficult to work without some sort of a team relationship when expensive facilities are needed (as in some visual or plastic arts or music). The ways advisors work with each other necessarily find their way into the ways we work with our graduate students. For advisors who publish with their students as well as with colleagues, I would like to share some thoughts and experiences. For those to whom the idea is strange, perhaps there may be some germs of useful ideas in these notes.

At the completion of a research doctoral degree, students will be faced with a number of potential occupational choices. Traditionally, doctoral degrees prepared future academicians and professors, but the majority of doctoral graduates are now found elsewhere in the work world. For example, some work in government and intergovernmental agencies, nongovernmental organizations, research and development branches of industry, grants offices and foundations, journalism, and active politics. The multiple roles that doctoral graduates find they must master increase regularly in number and complexity. Students' formal programs or courses of study may not have prepared them for all these possibilities. Advisors are often in an excellent position to progressively increase opportunities and responsibility to participate in the diversified opportunities that are come our way. The most immediately recognizable of these roles—and the one we can make a point of being most helpful in—is publishing, whether the student will publish as a sole author or in joint authorship with the advisor.

In some European universities and disciplines, a doctorate is awarded only after a dissertation has been published in book form. This has led to an industry of vanity presses that

will produce, at a price, as few beautifully bound copies as
needed of anyone's dissertation. Many North American and
perhaps other graduates receive invitations from these and
other firms to publish their work with them—employees of
these enterprising companies search the web for lists of new
doctoral graduates around the world. One of the continuing
contributions an advisor can make is to warn students not to
respond to these offers—to just click and delete the e-mail.
A dissertation in original form is rarely if ever worthy of direct publication. Some programs require that a comprehensive
examination paper be in the form of a publication, or allow
a dissertation to be series of linked publications with a common introduction and conclusion, but a formal requirement
that a student must actually publish a peer-reviewed scholarly
paper based on the thesis in order to graduate is exceedingly
rare. Without a publication record, however, possibly including items as sole or lead author in a manner appropriate to the
discipline, scholarships will be scarce, and a postdoctoral fellowship or research-related job will be hard to find, even if the
degree requirements were completed satisfactorily.

Advisors can take several steps to help students become
published by the time they graduate and to increase the prob-
ability—never a certainty—that graduates will continue to
publish. The preliminary step, before even accepting to advise, is to state that this is one of the expectations, the process
begins immediately, and it becomes increasingly cumulative,
complex, and independent over time. For better or worse,
publication plays an influential part in the building of a reputation as a knowledge creator. Although it should also be
clear that quality counts, it is appropriate to look at different
quantitative indices of accomplishment—for example, total

publication counts, impact indices, or citation counts—and to address their strengths and weaknesses. These topics might be discussed in a research-methods course, if the program has one, in a seminar, or in private.

There are occasionally situations in which it is proper to invite students to be additional authors on papers already in progress, based on mutually agreed-upon contributions to the work. This is especially helpful in the earlier phases of advising. These can include building or refining the review of past research, editing, data gathering or organizing, statistical or qualitative analyses, selecting an appropriate journal, and substantially editing or adapting manuscripts for paper or electronic submission, for example, creating a copy for "blind review" if that is required. A plan can be made for student engagement in publications, looking ahead about a year at a time, and discussing what roles the student can gradually assume so as to move toward the sole or premier position in the author list—the usual first occasion of this is work derived from the dissertation, but there are disciplinary differences. Most universities and several professional and academic associations have clear guidelines.

I tell my students that the element of greatest consequence in authorship order for multiply authored writing is whose idea the paper addresses. We build from there. I like to look at each project, including most theses, and to actively search for an interesting contribution to knowledge that originated with the student and one that came from me. We then work on more than one paper, if not simultaneously, then in close sequential order. I also tell students that at any time I welcome their proposals for a future publication. Finally, nearly every conference presentation by a student should contribute in some way to an ensuing refereed publication or a book chapter. In some disciplines the advisor's primary collaboration may take the form of helping the student make an independent contribution rather than negotiating joint efforts, but there is a common goal: advisors should scaffold students in their role as emerging scholars contributing to their field through publication.

Book chapters vary in popularity across different disciplines. Edited books are, for example, very common in the learning sciences and cognitive psychology. Because I work in part in that area, as my career progressed, invitations to contribute became more common. One filter I apply to each invitation is whether or not it is a good fit to what one or more of my students are doing. More often than not, students are first authors in these efforts. In one case it was possible to adapt and shorten the literature review of a dissertation to fit into a volume, because the review provided a new insight into the topic.

Authored books are often very personal statements reflecting years of work, sometimes across generations of students. I have not yet coauthored a book with a student, but I have employed students as editors to help get a volume into shape, especially a volume of invited chapters, and particularly with regard to formatting, reference cross-checking, and looking for newer or more relevant references. Two students have helped considerably in the revising of a particular chapter. This work is always acknowledged in the table of contents or acknowledgments of the volume. These skills are easily transferred to students' own work, although it is sometimes necessary to remind them to do so.

Publication collaboration can continue after some students graduate. My experience is that in most cases it drops off over the first two or three years after graduation, but it has provided a helpful running start for the student. Usually these items arise from the dissertation. With a very small number of former students, collaboration in authorship has continued for a long time because we retained common interests. This is never the expectation, just an occasional happy outcome. Preparing students for independent scholarship means just that, and eventually nearly all create their own new scholarly agendas and collegial links.

Mentoring

Most students leave following graduation and simply excel at what they do. A few choose to maintain a close relationship, one in which the advisor can suitably be described as a mentor. Every relationship should be enjoyed while it lasts to whatever degree. There can be no expectation of continuation.

The term *mentoring* is getting somewhat diluted. It now widely refers to any level of support offered to a newer member of a group. Academic departments have mentoring committees that help new professors choose priorities, prepare tenure applications, or plan effective teaching. The function phases out. However, sometimes a more senior colleague connects with a new department member and the sharing of concerns and priorities continues throughout a career, even if sporadically. The term *mentor* once had specific meaning. It came from Homer's *Iliad* and *Odyssey*. When Odysseus (Ulysses) departed for the Trojan wars, he asked his friend Mentor to care for his son Telemachus's well-being and education. Odysseus asked Mentor to personally invest in Telemachus, introduce him to society, open doors to opportunities, and provide guidance.

We do not know how much choice Telemachus or his mother had in the arrangement, and he was twenty years old when his father returned. Mutual choice is, however, part of adult mentorships. The beneficiary of a mentorship is referred to as the protégé, literally the protected.

Mentorship is related to the current notion of tutor or guardian. Interestingly, the French word for tutoring is *mentorat*. A mentorship, then, is a long-term connection that begins when the mentee is in a state of some dependence, but he or she grows to maturity and continues to take selective advantage of the mentor's experience at key junctures in life. It is possible to provide poor general advice or research guidance. A mentoring relationship is necessarily good or it is something else. Roles include guiding, modeling, teaching, protecting, and being a special friend. This last term is used with specific meaning in reflective practice and continuing professional development, including teaching, to refer to a colleague who serves as close advisor, a person with whom to share confidences and who will give honest answers every time—providing facial tissues as needed.

A mentoring relationship can become a mutually supportive connection. The caring element expands for both participants, with the mentee eventually caring for the mentor and the mentor happily being on the receiving end. I have had three people in my life whom I especially felt to be mentors and with whom a connection lasted or has lasted for decades. The first was my childhood piano teacher. I learned a relevant lesson decades ago when I asked how he knew when he had done a good job as a teacher. He replied that he succeeded not when his students were merely up to his standard and knowledge but when they had been catapulted well beyond, largely by their own interest and efforts. Despite my never reaching that standard, we are still friends and he does not consider himself a failure in my case! I have tried to make his definition part of how I support students' mature roles. I especially learned from him that as teachers we should celebrate when our students do not merely catch up to our knowledge and skill but exceed us in every possible way. The person who became my MA advisor provided many lessons, among which I particularly remember being encouraged to examine problems in unconventional ways. My longest-serving department chair alerted an eager young professor to choose his battles carefully and calmly let lesser priorities pass as they would. I sense the role exchange that occurred between each of them (two are still very much alive) and me in simple gestures such as the occasional phone call, a brief visit, or a trip to a coffee shop to keep up. And in my repeating their advice. A more concrete example was asking my former music teacher, who became an international performance coach, to write a book chapter and, with the help of one of my doctoral students and my daughter, guiding him in the discipline of putting big ideas into concise words, with no eighty-eight-note keyboard on which to demonstrate.

I think I have that bonus relationship with a handful of my hundred current and former graduate students. In the middle there are warm, how-wonderful-to-see-you connections with perhaps a quarter of the others, and the rest have done what is expected of them: get on with their lives. The graduates and soon-to-be graduates who may see me as mentor and not just past advisor come to do so gradually, and it is a mutual realization. I do not think the advisory relationship itself was any better or worse in these cases. Mentoring fills personal as well as professional needs, it is reciprocal, and it can be handed on across generations.

From time to time mentorship involves direct scholarly collaboration. I have reached out to past students, and they sometimes call me for help with an article or chapter, or to give a guest seminar should they be teaching at the postsecondary level. Typical points of professional interaction include being consulted about whether to take that tempting position near a beach halfway around the world, getting together at conferences, looking over a manuscript, preparing a grant, and writing a text.

Unique circumstances bring some students much closer to our personal lives than others. My wife and I have become almost surrogate parents for some. We have been invited to weddings, held baby showers, recommended our personal banker, and consoled students following the collapse of a relationship. Some of this subgroup of advisees became family friends. But we have enough fingers, perhaps on one hand, to tally the total number of advisees now in this category. This continuing relationship is a wonderful addition; it is not an essential benchmark of successful advising. Not all advising is mentoring in the classic sense of the word.

When mentoring evolves into a reciprocally satisfying situation, of course there can be unexpected consequences. All advisors are aware that having competent graduate students amplifies our own professional productivity. What also appears to happen in the development of student-centered advising, and even more strongly among those that evolve into mentoring relationships, is that students come to think well of their advisors as people. Perhaps not all of us are terribly concerned about this outcome; after all, our job is shaping up

these new academic minds. I suggest, however, that the collegial relationship, the one that can evolve into future colleagueship, brings benefits to advisors that should not be waved off.
Feeling good is good.

Finally, like advising, mentorship is neither ownership nor
exclusive. A graduate student or graduate can and should comfortably have multiple mentors. A conference presentation
about the genealogy of one of my areas of research traced who
in the field had studied with whom and enabled me to pon-
der at a new level how the research had evolved: if scholars are
the products of superior advising, strong new branches on the
family tree of scholarship are the products of mentorship.

6

INSTITUTIONALIZING A CULTURE OF STUDENT-CENTERED ADVISING

Physics teaches us that changing direction or velocity requires external input. To strengthen student-centered advising, we must apply new forces. The preceding chapters especially addressed individual advisors and students. The graduate experience is local; however, it is governed institutionally and shaped by society. Students interact with each other and know that advising comes in many flavors. We advisors perpetuate our own experiences (or not, recalling the student who became determined not to be a "slave driver" when she had her own advisees). Change requires actions beyond those of individual advisors.

I have some suggestions for how administrative units and universities as a whole can support the culture and practice of student-centered advising. These are not templates but a collection of ideas that might promote useful conversation among faculty members, graduate students, administrators, and policy makers. A few general principles preface this advice.

First, student-centered advising does not thrive in a vacuum, or without support in terms of goals, strategies, shared positive experiences, and opportunity to reflect and compare notes with colleagues in an evaluation-free context. Implicit support is better than none. Explicit support is better. Second, the *context* needs to emulate what student-centered advising tries to be: not entirely top-down or bottom-up, but a respectful, dynamic combination. It must enhance the individual advisor, the unit, and the institution as a whole. Institutions that set the goal of creating, building, or enhancing the graduate experience of their students—a frequently stated goal—might experiment with these ideas. Third, eliminate any taboos about any of the topics addressed in this book—they all need to be discussed.

But what do you do if your chair and dean are hostile to the idea of student-centered advising? What if the culture of the department or even the university is that the great students will swim and the merely good ones will sink, and that's fine with everyone? There are no easy answers, but an individual supervisor can follow most of the advice in this book without making waves, and in such circumstances it might be a good idea to get tenure before trying to change the institution or its culture. Assume that this will be a slow process. It might begin with a small, informal monthly gathering of like-minded advisors. A graduate students' association might take up the conversation or organize recognition events such as mentoring awards. If there is a teaching-improvement service, that unit might prepare a briefing paper and take other initiatives. And there is always the question of cost: having graduate students fall by the wayside, especially after the first year has passed, is expensive in terms of supervision time from faculty and financial support spent on students who do not complete their studies. Somehow, somewhere, discreetly among colleagues or in conversation with a sympathetic member of the governing board if not a willing chair, dean, or provost, plant the seed.

Unit Initiatives

Using student and peer nominations, departments and centers can identify advisors consistently recognized as creating student-centered relationships with their students. Ask these advisors to post suggestions about their approaches on a section of the departmental website devoted to teaching and supervision suggestions, and to serve on advisory committees with new faculty members, perhaps as coadvisors, with an explicit mandate to support the advisory process.

Create a working group of students and professors to periodically review departmental and student handbooks and websites, look for opportunities to strengthen communication of these goals, address elements of practice, and offer an annual or more frequent award (even a simple piece of paper) to advisors who exhibit student-centered qualities—such positive reinforcement of good mentoring also motivates others to invest more in their students. Ensure that procedures are clear about what steps students should take when they have difficulty with their advisors. Each year at orientation sessions, mention that the department values and promotes positive advisory experiences, and highlight some of the qualities students should expect. Class committees of a few students elected by their peers (with the instructor temporarily out of the room) are sometimes needed to communicate suggestions from students about improving the class or resolving difficulties. A similar mechanism could be used at the graduate level. There should be at least two student members of this group (for safety in numbers). Communication should be informal, without a paper trail, directly with the program director or chair, and gatherings held about once a month with the option of extra meetings as needed—scheduled meetings reduce the impression that students come only to complain.

Some universities require the chair, director, or dean to meet annually with faculty members to review their accomplishments, and especially with professors on the path to a tenure application. These meetings typically address course teaching, publications, grant support, and service through committees or participation in professional or academic associations. Faculty members typically might be asked global questions about the numbers of students they are actively advising and how close they are to graduation. The chair or dean could also make clear that student-centered advising is a priority by meeting with advisors once or twice a year to go over their particular students in more than cursory detail. However, the discussion about each student needs to go beyond a quick statement of satisfactory progress. What are the student's strengths? Has the student encountered any serious obstacles? What steps have been taken to bring this student closer to being a colleague? These would be individual private meetings, different from the program meetings, for example, that we have in our department in which professors meet as a group to review students' annual reports of progress. Units can also collect exit feedback from graduates at the time of graduation, or soon after, about their experiences in their degree and where their career is heading.

Appendix 3 contains a checklist, based on the topics of this book, that advisors and advisees can use or adapt to follow their progress toward student-centered supervision. The

list can also be useful as a menu for workshops or discussion
groups addressing the various topics at the departmental or
institutional level.

Institutional Initiatives

At senior academic committees, schedule conversations about
the qualities of good advising. My university's senate receives
an annual report from the ombudsperson for students, and
some related topics arise there, but this is not the same as time
in "committee of the whole" devoted to an open conversation.
Expect movement to be gradual. Start using the language, but
words without related action generate cynicism.

Graduate schools, teaching-development services, or faculty
associations can draw on identified student-centered advisors
as seminar animators and as presenters or panelists to contribute to information sessions and short workshops around the
campus. Graduate students and faculty members should be
welcome at such sessions, and students could be part of the
organizing teams. If particular faculty members are enlisted
frequently, along with additional coadvising requests, consider
creating a rotating pool of funds for a few years to reimburse
units for some course-teaching release to make it easier for
these colleagues to be available during the semester. Professors enjoy interacting with colleagues from other parts of the
university. Cross-disciplinary dialogue helps ensure that ideas
particular or foreign to any part of the university—for example, individual scholarship, research teams, group supervision,
copublishing or never copublishing with students, sharing or
never sharing the contents of reference letters—are reinter-
preted among colleagues within the institution in ways that

can make wider good sense. Practices such as research teams comprising faculty members, technicians, and graduate students are "normal" for some science advisors, who might rarely if ever have experienced being the only important campus contact as for a humanities student. These discussions can also be valuable forums for discussion of potential bias in institutional favor of one form of knowledge production over another, even if major funding agencies have already declared themselves on such matters. Faculty members who become familiar with the range of advisory realities in a university can also be in a better and more trusted position to take leadership positions that cut across disciplines. A short book like this one that raises interpersonal advising issues with examples can only raise the topics for a local audience to elaborate in relevant ways. But most of the advice directly cuts across domains.

Student-centered advising can be described on the graduate studies web page, and relevant policies can be linked. Review policies and procedures to ensure that they protect students and identify safe places for them to discuss their concerns and get help. Although serious consequences are warranted for severe misconduct, punishment is a very poor motivational device when learning is the goal. Punishment reinforces avoidance among faculty members as well as students, and the instant punitive impulse of some student and staff disciplinary codes probably does not achieve the desired outcomes.

Criteria for advising and graduate teaching awards can be tied to some of the ideas central to student-centered advising. Nomination letters over the years can be searched for statements that highlight the kinds of advisory actions and attitudes that students have highly valued. These unattributed statements can be presented on the graduate studies web page

and in a brochure sent annually to faculty members and graduate students. Finally, many companies conduct exit interviews
with employees who resign in order to learn why they are leaving and how retention can be improved. With a third to a half
of doctoral students not finishing their degree (generally caring about students is not enough to remedy this), much valuable information would be gained by a confidential interview,
even if only some of the departing students participated. Only
some of the questions would address advising, but the formal
knowledge base is so far rather anecdotal.

Policies that require students to submit annual progress reports and plans for the next year, both countersigned
by the advisor, can be extended to require annual conversations—such as proposed above—between unit administrators
and individual advisors about the progress of each advisee. If
requiring such conversations is distasteful in the already ex-
tensively regulated world of universities, then recommend it
and provide some incentive for units that do it. Incentives can
range from public recognition to a couple of hundred dollars
for the unit to hold a year-end social event, such as a wine and
cheese or coffee hour, for faculty members and graduate students together. Or make it a centrally offered event.

Some universities, including my own, have appointed
staff to conduct formal professional development activities for
graduate students addressing a number of the topics raised in
this book and others, and at school or department levels doctoral students have been hired to organize a series of seminars
and workshops to promote graduate student success across disciplines. These are highly worthy enterprises that could also
address some of the more sensitive topics mentioned in this
book. They have the potential to create dialogue among ad-

ministrators, faculty members, and students on these topics without the pressure of focusing on any one relationship.

Student-centered advising involves knowledge, action, and attitude. The critical focus is on the relationship between the individual advisor and student. Making student-centered advising the everyday experience of every faculty member and student also depends on commitment and action by immediate colleagues and the institution as a whole.

Do It Right

Many advisors are survivors of sink-or-swim experiences, including graduate school. We even take some pride in having made it, and some of us assume that running our advisees through the same gauntlet will make them better graduates. It does not. Rather, it wastes talent, creates negative memories about the institution (the office of development—an interesting name for fundraising—would not be pleased), it can harm lives, and it makes inefficient use of financial resources. It is punishment, and therefore it contributes to students' dropping out. Even if it appears that no one else has taken a student-centered approach to advising, and the local culture is not currently supportive, it is ultimately a benefit to advisors and students, and to the unit and institution.

A transition toward student-centered advising does not happen on its own. It requires the application of motivation and direction. The benefits of positive graduate experiences of students and advisors, and the ensuing advantages for the unit and institution, are good reasons to do it right.

APPENDIX I

Additional Reading

There are no other books that give direct advice in the manner of the present volume. This is a very select list, therefore, of a small number of other references that address related topics, sometimes making points that I agree with, and sometimes points I reject. I have found them interesting, and at the very least they contributed to my choice of topics. There are no references in this list that are exclusively about how to produce or guide students toward a successful dissertation. Each at least partially addresses the human interactions that are the focus of this book.

Bartlett, A., and G. Mercer, eds. 2001. *Postgraduate Research Supervision: Transforming (R)elations*. New York: Peter Lang. 284 pp. This book focuses on a range of Australian narratives from the perspective of the advisee, but with little direct advice for supervisors. Except for one experience with instructional technology, all the reports are from the humanities and social sciences, and the contributed chapters are primarily personal stories with a strong feminist voice. The experiences of women as graduate students are especially interesting for understanding the impact of power differentials, as well as for the reasons they undertook graduate studies. Among the useful topics are fear of recrimination for challenging the authority of the supervisor (chap. 1), the difference between supervision of theses and of students (chap. 2), and the importance of the supervisory relationship in general (especially see chaps. 1, 10, and 20). Chapter 15 is particularly controversial, suggesting that consensual sexual relations should not be addressed by harassment policies and might be acceptable, such as between a supervisor and student who are both mature, experienced professionals, and that the conflict of interest lies only in the evaluation process, not the research advising. In contrast, I have proposed that sexual relations should indeed be treated in conflict-of-interest policies and such compartmentalization is not really possible. Chapter 22 led me to the Hockey 1996 reference in this list. The volume also has an extensive and useful reference list.

Gordon, V. N., W. R. Habley, T. J. Crites, and associates. eds. 2008. *Academic Advising: A Comprehensive Handbook.* 2nd ed. Manhattan, KS: National Academic Advising Association / San Francisco, CA: Jossey-Bass. This book provides a US-based perspective on the process of being a graduate student and addresses the history of advising in universities, ethics, legal issues, and different kinds of universities. It especially draws attention to the importance of sensitivity to students' personal situations and success.

Hockey, J. 1996. "A Contractual Solution to Problems in the Supervision of PhD Degrees in the UK." *Studies in Higher Education* 21:359–71. Hockey documents the value of a nego-tiated "written contract between supervisor and student, and the foundations of this form of agreement . . . followed by a proposed outline for such a contract . . . a strategy rarely utilised or even considered in the process of research student supervision" (359). The article especially focuses on sustaining student motivation, and it reports that "the majority of supervisory relationships were conducted in relaxed fashion, with the use of first names by both parties, and with work schedules and programmes agreed orally" (364). If, however, "problematic situations develop after the establishment of such a contract, it can then always be cited as the formal agreement which has been generated to structure conduct and as a validation for sanctions should they be needed" (364). The contract is adapted for each student, different disciplines, et cetera. My own experience is that timelines cannot be realistically laid out at the outset, but a good approximation of forthcoming deadlines can be done annually and modified as needed. I like Hockey's main point that there should be "agreements of a general nature pertaining to the dynamics of supervision" (366) and "what is required of the supervisor is to be as clear and honest as possible about the nature of the supervisory relationship and the work" (368).

McAlpine, L., and J. Norton. 2006. "Reframing Our Approach to Doctoral Programs: An Integrative Framework for Action and Research." *Higher Education Research and Development* 25, no. 1: 3–17. doi:10.1080/07294360500453012. This article points out that the attrition rate in doctoral programs hovers around 50 percent, reflecting a terrible waste of talent and effort. As part of a study of doctoral attrition, McAlpine and Norton systematically reviewed one hundred studies of attrition in doctoral programs to better understand the reasons for noncompletion. Dropping out was typically attributed to personal characteristics of the students, and institutional contributions were not acknowledged. This was a benchmark contribution and pointed to key issues involved in advising at multiple levels—dyadic, local institutional, and societal.

Peters, R. L. 1997. *Getting What You Came For: The Smart Student's Guide to Earning a Master's or Ph.D.* Rev. ed. New York: Farrar, Straus and Giroux / Macmillan. Process-focused, as are most of the other available books, this volume includes a chapter on the importance of choosing an advisor who will mentor well, managing or navigating academic politics, and coping with professorial hostility. The other chapters are mostly about writing and defending an excellent dissertation, plus job search.

Thornton, R. J. 2003. *Lexicon of Intentionally Ambiguous Recommendations (LIAR).* Naperville, IL: Sourcebooks. Originally published in 1988, this tongue-in-cheek guide to writing reference letters is actually useful as a reminder that we must be judicious in how we refer to our students, especially in avoiding unintentional ambiguities when writing reference letters. My favorite sentence appears on the cover of the 2003 printing: "You will be very lucky to get this man to work for you."

Wisker, G. 2005. *The Good Supervisor: Supervising Postgraduate and Undergraduate Research for Doctoral Theses and Dissertations.* Palgrave Study Guides. Houndmills, Basingstoke, UK: Palgrave Macmillan. Although student-sensitive, this book like most others is focused on the tasks of doing a thesis. It is especially relevant to supervision in the humanities and social sciences. Of particular interest to the relationship between advisor and student, the book especially attended to creating communities of learners (including students helping each other) and the special needs of international students. The book also introduces readers to unique features of English doctoral studies such as the "viva," and it contains an extensive reference list.

APPENDIX 2

Sample Contract for Graduate Advising:
Mutual Standards for Accountability

I have been using an evolving version of this contract for nearly four decades. Realization of the need to specify some of the key elements of the relationship with students came mostly from my having to explain this with each new supervisee and the inherent concern that I would not be consistent in doing so. Students also went on with their lives after graduation and sometimes lost contact; I wanted to see their work published but did not have access to the data or statistical analyses we had generated together. I once asked the students whether they thought this was redundant, but they advocated keeping it. Still, I do not personally know another professor who uses such a formal contract. It is not an unknown process (see Hockey 1996, appendix 1), but I join Hockey in recommending it strongly. This sample contract informs both new students and new supervisors about their mutual responsibilities. As Hockey noted, it can point to solutions when there are conflicts, and especially help us to avoid them.

One of the challenges in working with a contract such as this is the level of specificity, for example, regarding the frequency of meetings. This simply cannot be specified over the years of a supervision relationship. At times "regularly" can mean anything from weekly to a few times a year, and not always in person, depending on how smoothly work is advancing or whether or not the student is on campus. To me, "regular" has meant often enough to ensure reasonably steady progress, and the intervals can be varied as needed. At times the student or I will ask for more or more frequent meetings, and sometimes students or I suggest a string of weekly meetings to overcome current hurdles.

Some items in this sample contract may be irrelevant for some disciplines, such as references to team activities (item B2), and some points essential in others are clearly missing (such as interactions with laboratory staff or patients in the health sciences). Several items in this sample contract are illustrative, not prescriptive. Others should apply widely. It is intended to be adapted to local need, not photocopied and handed out. Indeed, a conversation among faculty members and students, or between an advisor and her or his advisees, could be very helpful for creating a first draft and updating the contract as needed.

MUTUAL EXPECTATIONS REGARDING
RESEARCH ADVISING

High Ability and Inquiry Research Group
DEPARTMENT OF EDUCATIONAL AND COUNSELLING
PSYCHOLOGY, MCGILL UNIVERSITY

These notes are designed as guidelines to facilitate positive and mutually beneficial student-advisor relationships and to avoid problems on matters such as authorship and credits on publications, the extent of participation in activities other than the Thesis, Research Project, or Special Activity, and future access to data collected in the course of our work together. Some of the activities described below may be conducted in groups. Where these notes hinder rather than help, they should be amended to meet mutually acceptable needs, in general or as occasions arise.

A. Advisor's Responsibilities
   1. Meet regularly with students and be contactable at other times.
   2. Arrange substitute advising during extended absences.
   3. Advise on course selection.
   4. Assist in the preparation for comprehensive or oral examinations.
   5. Help prepare conference and journal presentations based on work done in the program and assist with applications for support to attend suitable conferences at a reasonable distance and on whose programs students earn a place.
   6. Help apply for funds to cover direct research costs and to provide stipends to full-time students.

7. Provide feedback within a mutually agreed time-frame on written work submitted for review.

B. Students' Responsibilities

1. Regularly pursue work and keep the advisor informed of progress or problems.

2. To a mutually agreed degree that respects other responsibilities and priorities, contribute to advancing team activities that further the common good of all of us working together—e.g., workshops for teachers, parent contacts, library orders, data bases, maintaining bibliographies and mailing lists, convening meetings, maintaining computers and supplies. These tasks will be equitably distributed.

3. Join in the preparation of conference presentations and publications on research and other activities done with faculty members.

4. With appropriate guidance, prepare a draft version of the thesis or major report, normally within 3 months of its final presentation for master's degrees, or 6 months for doctoral degrees; after that point the advisor may take over such preparation and the order of authorship may be changed (within CPA, APA and McGill authorship guidelines).

5. Apply for scholarships and bursaries, especially FQRSC, McGill, and SSHRC (where eligible) [this list of funding sources should be amended to match local availability].

6. Participate to a mutually agreed extent in teaching-related activities such as the TA course.

7. Take a professional role in one's discipline by undertaking at least one student or regular membership in an appropriate professional or academic organization.

8. Keep at McGill a copy of raw data, coding sheets, instruments, and subject-identification data.

9. Upon graduation, leave with the advisor a printed copy of the main research report, and an electronic copy in modifiable form (e.g., not PDF) of any data and the text of the thesis or project.

10. Use Microsoft Word and APA [or other, as appropriate] style for written submissions.

11. Report annually in writing on progress and contributions (department and university forms).

12. Regularly attend and participate in research-team meetings.

C. Joint Responsibilities

1. Give full credit for the contributions of others and to research funding in all products.

2. Assign authorship according to the latest APA publication guidelines. (For example, if a thesis topic or report is entirely the student's original contribution, then the advisor's contribution is due a footnote. Shared scientific responsibility calls for co-authorship, with the student as first author on the main points of the student's research of those for which the student took primary creative responsibility, and the advisor as first author on any specific subpoints which the advisor contributed or a broader study of which the student is part.)

3. Both have unlimited access to the data collected on or about the topic of a thesis or project during the time worked together, plus any other that may be agreed to, giving due credit to its origin either by footnote or by reference to previous publications.

D. Degree Covered by This Agreement

Check-mark all that apply [and revise this list as needed for your institution]:

❏ PhD Thesis or Dissertation

❏ MA Thesis

❏ MA Research Project

❏ MEd "Special Activity" Project

❏ Undergraduate Honors Thesis

❏ Independent Graduate Student Project

❏ Independent Undergraduate Student Project

❏ Other (specify): _____

_____

❏ Not for formal credit

E. Comments, Additions, or Special Notes [expand this space as required]

F. Signatures

We agree to work together in an advisory relationship in accord with the above guidelines.

_____   _____

Advisor   Date   Student   Date

_____   _____

Printed Name   Printed Name

One copy for each.

APPENDIX 3

Student-Centered Advising Checklist

Do I agree with the general idea of student-centered advising? Am I a student-centered advisor? How are we doing as a group? Use this checklist item by item or as a whole. More importantly, however, it can help advisors answer the question, "Am I now more student-centered than I was a year ago?" Another possible group use could be as an expanded menu, similar to the table of contents, for topics to be addressed in workshops or discussion groups about quality graduate and other advising, or for a program or unit (rather than individuals, who in this case could reply anonymously) to gauge the unit's progress toward student-centered supervision. This checklist could be mentioned to graduate students who might come across this book. It might be helpful to committees selecting winners of supervision awards or to writers of reference letters for advisors. It might even be a potentially useful research tool. Feel free to adapt it to your local needs (an acknowledgment of the source or inspiration is always appreciated). You are welcome to photocopy or scan this appendix for the above uses.

For each statement, circle + if you agree, o if you are undecided or neutral, or − if you disagree.

From chapter #	Some examples of student-centered graduate research supervision: a personal portrait *These items cover only a sample of the advice offered in this volume, and without the nuances expressed in the text. Changes, additions, or deletions to the items to local circumstances are invited.*	I generally support this advice:			This advice reflects my actions with my advisees:		
1	Prospective advisees and advisors should discuss their strengths, preferences, and expectations.	+	o	–	+	o	–
	Financial support should be discussed before mutually agreeing to supervision.	+	o	–	+	o	–
	Advisors should be clear about their comfort with students' getting experience in other labs or groups.	+	o	–	+	o	–
	Advisors should be able to articulate their supervisory style or model.	+	o	–	+	o	–
	The supervision decision should be mutually agreed upon.	+	o	–	+	o	–
2	Advisors benefit when students are treated respectfully.	+	o	–	+	o	–
	Advisees should have a strong sense of ownership of their dissertation topic.	+	o	–	+	o	–
	Advisors should respond sensitively to variations in students' progress or health.	+	o	–	+	o	–
	Confidences shared by students are strictly private.	+	o	–	+	o	–

From chapter #	Some examples of student-centered graduate research supervision: a personal portrait *These items cover only a sample of the advice offered in this volume, and without the nuances expressed in the text. Changes, additions, or deletions to the items to local circumstances are invited.*	I generally support this advice:			This advice reflects my actions with my advisees:		
	Advisors should respond to written submissions as quickly as possible, rarely taking as long as two weeks maximum.	+	o	−	+	o	−
	Advisors should respond promptly to requests to schedule meetings or conversations.	+	o	−	+	o	−
	Advisors should expect to guide advisees through difficult or complex steps.	+	o	−	+	o	−
	Students should provide written reports at least annually of their progress along milestones of the degree.	+	o	−	+	o	−
3	Advisors' significant others need to know students with whom the advisor works, and vice versa.	+	o	−	+	o	−
	Advisors should actively help advisees not become overloaded and help them moderate their commitments.	+	o	−	+	o	−
	Advisors should help students with suitable words when students need to say no to a request.	+	o	−	+	o	−

From chapter #	Some examples of student-centered graduate research supervision: a personal portrait *These items cover only a sample of the advice offered in this volume, and without the nuances expressed in the text. Changes, additions, or deletions to the items to local circumstances are invited.*	I generally support this advice:			This advice reflects my actions with my advisees:		
	Advisors should be sensitive to students' comfort level in forms of address and greeting.	+	o	–	+	o	–
	Advisors should ensure that subtle language or humor is understood by students with diverse language backgrounds.	+	o	–	+	o	–
	When entertaining students at home, advisors should always include a cohost and end the party at the same time for all students.	+	o	–	+	o	–
	Socializing with students should be done publicly, normally in groups of three or more.	+	o	–	+	o	–
	The default for physical contact with an advisee is none, and permission should be asked even for required contact.	+	o	–	+	o	–
	When students underperform, compassionately ask about the specific concern before focusing on the negative.	+	o	–	+	o	–
	Devote time, perhaps in groups, to addressing professional and life skills such as professional dress and speech.	+	o	–	+	o	–

From chapter #	Some examples of student-centered graduate research supervision: a personal portrait *These items cover only a sample of the advice offered in this volume, and without the nuances expressed in the text. Changes, additions, or deletions to the items to local circumstances are invited.*	I generally support this advice:			This advice reflects my actions with my advisees:		
4	Students do not need to know the details of problematic relationships among professorial colleagues.	+	o	−	+	o	−
	Students stranded without an advisor should be helped in their search for a new one.	+	o	−	+	o	−
	An advisor should treat multiple advisees equitably.	+	o	−	+	o	−
	Advisees should be guided in learning to discriminate between excellent and perfect work on their part.	+	o	−	+	o	−
	Advisees need guidance in setting achievable goals and breaking difficult tasks into smaller, doable parts.	+	o	−	+	o	−
	Advisors do not need to know very personal details about students, unless they interfere with satisfactory progress.	+	o	−	+	o	−
	Conflicts of interest such as family, financial, or friendship connections should be declared and removed.	+	o	−	+	o	−
	Advisors must never have sex with an advisee or any student for whom they have academic responsibilities.	+	o	−	+	o	−

From chapter #	Some examples of student-centered graduate research supervision: a personal portrait	I generally support this advice:			This advice reflects my actions with my advisees:		
	These items cover only a sample of the advice offered in this volume, and without the nuances expressed in the text. Changes, additions, or deletions to the items to local circumstances are invited.						
5	Advisees should have opportunities to participate in proposing and delivering conference presentations, teaching, reviewing manuscripts, and consulting.	+	o	–	+	o	–
	Advisees should be asked if there is something they especially want included in a reference letter, but not asked to write the letter.	+	o	–	+	o	–
	Advisees should be assisted in publishing their dissertations or parts thereof, but never in a vanity press.	+	o	–	+	o	–
6	Departments should have clear procedures that students should follow when they have difficulty with their advisors.	+	o	–	+	o	–
	Universities and graduate schools should ensure that advisor-advisee relationships are openly addressed in official communications and practices.	+	o	–	+	o	–
Total 1	Support profile for student-centered advising (total frequency for these 3 columns):				x	x	x
Total 2	Practice profile for student-centered advising (total frequency for these 3 columns):	x	x	x			

INDEX

teaching, x, 16, 26, 27, 33, 42, 43, 56,
58, 64, 107, 109, 110, 111, 124–25, 130,
131, 144, 152
teaching improvement service, 12, 88, 129
teams, research, vii, 14, 145
tears, 67, 69, 70, 93, 97, 124
thank-you letters, 17
thesis, ix, 21, 24, 27, 148
touching students, 64–67, 150

university administration, ix, x, 64–65,
80, 84, 129
university culture, ix, xi, 128–35
university or institutional initiatives to
promote student-centered advising,
132–35, 152

wanderers (students serially linked to
advisors), 82–85